Baltic Sea

North Sea

HAMBURG

BREMEN

KYRITZ (SCHLOSS KARNZOW)

POZNAN

AMSTERDAM

NETHERLANDS

HANNOVER

GRASLEBEN

BERLIN

POLAND

BERNTERODE

DÜSSELDORF

LEIPZIG

SIEGEN

MARBURG

MERKERS

DRESDEN

BRUSSELS

AACHEN

GROSSCOTTA

BELGIUM

KOBLENZ

WIESBADEN

FRANKFURT

PRAGUE

OFFENBACH

LUX.

CZECHOSLOVAKIA

METZ

HEILBRONN

NUREMBERG

FRANCE

STUTTGART

ELLINGEN

GERMANY

LINZ

MUNICH

AUSTRIA

VIENNA

ZURICH

BERCHTESGADEN

FÜSSEN (NEUSCHWANSTEIN CASTLE)

ALT AUSSEE

SWITZERLAND

BOLZANO

ITALY

EUROPE: LATE 1945

★ ALLIED COLLECTING POINT

⚡ NAZI REPOSITORY

MASTERPIECE ON THE MOVE

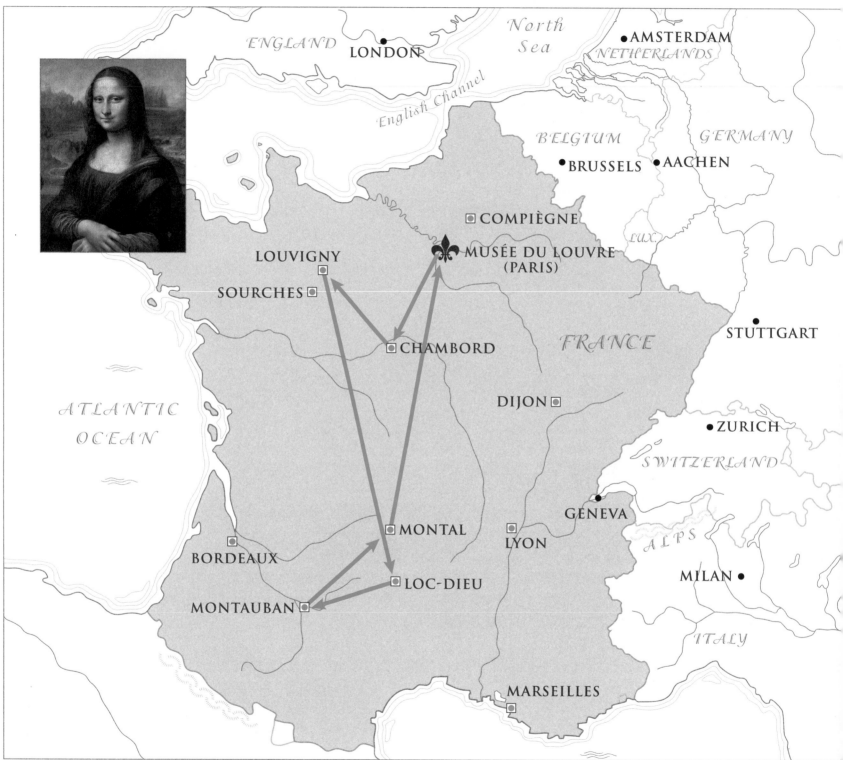

Perhaps the most recognizable work of art in the world, Leonardo da Vinci's painting of the *Mona Lisa* was moved by French museum officials six times, beginning with its evacuation from the Louvre in September 1939, before its return to Paris on June 16, 1945.

RESCUING DA VINCI

LAUREL PUBLISHING, LLC
DALLAS

Vincent van Gogh,
The Sower, **1888.**
Oil on canvas, 64 x 80.5 cm
(25 ¼ × 31 ⅔ in).
Van Gogh Museum,
Amsterdam.

*"Anyone who sees and paints a sky green and
pastures blue ought to be sterilized."*

ADOLF HITLER

RESCUING DA VINCI

Hitler and the Nazis Stole Europe's Great Art
America and Her Allies Recovered It

ROBERT M. EDSEL

FOREWORDS BY
LYNN H. NICHOLAS AND EDMUND P. PILLSBURY, PH.D.

COVER

Major Estreicher, MFAA officer Lt. Frank P. Albright, and two American GIs marvel at *Lady With an Ermine*, one of Leonardo da Vinci's rescued masterworks.

Leonardo da Vinci, *Lady With an Ermine (Portrait of Cecilia Gallerani)*, c. 1483-88. Oil on panel, 55 × 40 cm (21 ⅔ × 15 ¾ in). Czartoryski Museum, Cracow.

editorial and design by j weikersheimer for rosebud books

imaging, prepress and printing by greg della stua for Americanbook.net in Singapore

ISBN 0-97743349-4-X

10 09 08 07 06

CONTENTS

"...Art is a human activity having as its aim to convey to people the highest and best feelings up to which mankind has lived...."

LEO TOLSTOY *WHAT IS ART?* 1898

Vatican Apartments

The galleries at the Vatican were reopened to the public. Among the first to enjoy its magnificent treasures were these United States servicemen and women, seen standing in a room with frescoes by the great Renaissance painter Raphael. The photograph above shows the room as it appears today.

FOREWORD *by Lynn H. Nicholas*

The history of war, and particularly that of World War II, is often distilled to numbers. We are told how many millions of people died, how many tons of bombs were dropped, how many billions of dollars were spent. Damage is expressed in monetary terms and, in the case of the displacement and destruction of art and monuments, much emphasis is placed on the value of what was taken, how much was recovered, and how much is still missing. In this flood of statistics the human reality of war and loss is soon swept away. Vivid verbal descriptions can certainly help to recreate the reality, but it is only through photographs that the full impact is brought home.

Looting has always been a part of warfare, but the magnitude of the operations of the Nazi art gathering agencies far surpassed anything previously attempted. Their actions were not merely stealing done in the heat of battle, but were ideological programs carefully linked to Nazi racial and genocidal programs. The national collections of nations considered to be Nordic were essentially left intact, while those of areas with "alien" populations, such as the Slavic regions, were stripped bare. Artifacts of alien cultures were destroyed, or preserved in special racial studies institutes as examples of what was to be eliminated. Anything "Germanic" found in the conquered lands of both East and West was, eventually, to be brought back to the fatherland. Private property, and especially that of Jews, though traditionally protected by the rules of warfare, was not exempt in this conflict, and would provide the bulk of Nazi requisitions in Western Europe. And all the millions of stolen objects, even when not acceptable according to Nazi theory, were, nevertheless, exploited with the greatest cynicism in European art markets.

At the end of the conflict, the vast stores of Nazi loot became the responsibility of the victorious armies. The responses of East and West were utterly different. In the East, the Soviet authorities removed both Nazi loot and German-owned works to the USSR feeling that it was justifiable restitution for the terrible losses they had suffered. Much was returned to the national collections of Eastern Bloc nations soon after the war, but much still remains in the former Soviet Union. It was the policy of the major Western allies to return looted items to the nations from which they had been taken and allow special commissions in each country to determine ownership. Securing, sorting, and identifying the millions of stolen objects found in the devastated reaches of the Third Reich was a complex and often dangerous process which would take the dedicated few assigned to such duties nearly seven years to achieve. Even after this huge effort, many works remained lost. Happily, due to renewed interest in closing this unfinished chapter of the Nazi era, many cases long thought to be hopeless, have been re-examined and hundreds of items returned in recent years to both national collections and individuals.

When *The Rape of Europa* was first published I knew that the photographs were essential to the understanding of its story, but in that long book, only a few of the images I had seen could be included. Since then, those working in the enormously expanded field of restitution and provenance research have found hundreds more images. Thanks to Robert Edsel and his extraordinary team of researchers, the best of these photographs have been retrieved and reproduced here, making them accessible at last to the general public. No one who has seen them will ever again view a peaceful museum collection or a historic building without being reminded of the vicissitudes which may have befallen it and marveling at the miracle of its survival.

It is to be hoped that this book will serve, not only as a record of the past, and as a salute to the dedicated men and women of all nations who risked their lives to save Europe's patrimony, but as a reminder of the destruction war brings to the fabric of human life. For the buildings and works of art, both public and private, which are lost in conflict are not just inanimate objects, but elements beloved by their owners and by the various cultures. The destruction and theft of such things, as the framers of the Hague Convention so clearly stated, violates the very soul of a people.

It is probably impossible to eliminate warfare entirely from future human history, but we can try, and by common agreement, we can act to preserve and respect cultural objects even in conflict. This book and its unforgettable images will surely help in that endeavor, and Robert Edsel is to be commended for commemorating here the terrible events of World War II and the heroic efforts of the "Monuments Men" to save Europe's artistic treasures.

Lynn H. Nicholas
Washington, D.C.

Sistine Chapel

Allied servicemen and women gather in the Sistine Chapel to enjoy a quiet and relaxing moment while observing the impressive ceiling frescoes (above). The color photograph provides an insight into the full genius of Michelangelo and his achievement.

"Humanity looks to works of art to shed light upon its path and its destiny."

POPE JOHN PAUL II

FOREWORD
by Edmund P. Pillsbury

The consequences of war are inevitably devastating in human terms—if death and injury are any measure—but they are no less severe in the realm of the loss and destruction of cultural property. Throughout history, spoils of war have featured objects of art, notably those of gold and silver but also traditional sculptures and paintings, as well as arms, armor, and bullion. Whether seized as reparations for real or perceived misdeeds, wantonly stolen to adorn the walls of a private palace or new museum as trophies of victory, or ostensibly borrowed for safekeeping in the interests of preservation, the enrichment of one culture often deprives another of its most tangible evidence of identity as a people. Art, if anything, constitutes the quest for truth and beauty; it records a pursuit of universal values that defines a society at any given time in history. To rob or destroy the patrimony of one civilization, particularly if done to glorify or enrich that of another, is tantamount to genocide, albeit bloodless. The endless public debates about cultural assets today and the ceaseless barrage of claims against governments and museums on both moral and legal grounds bear testimony to this reality.

There is no better instance of war's insidious impact upon its victims than the case of the last Great War—so poignantly described in print and now in film as *The Rape of Europa*. In fact, as Lynn Nicholas's scholarly chronicle of 1994 of that name brilliantly documents and as this stirring compilation of images and commentary so scrupulously brought together here by Robert Edsel illuminates, the tumultuous years of 1939 to 1945 witnessed the destruction and dislocation of cultural property on an unprecedented scale. Without so much as Jupiter's disguise as a bull to deceive his victims, Adolf Hitler embarked upon a mission to acquire the greatest works of art from ancient times to the present in private or public hands throughout the continent of Europe—a virtual who's who of the history of art—and the corollary purging of his own country's holdings of so-called degenerate (*entartete*) art by (ironically) some of Germany's most creative living talents. The property of Jewish families and Slavic peoples in Poland and Russia became the favorite targets of his calculated plunder, but few countries in Europe escaped the grasp of his minions, and the works of art that the Nazi forces removed from France and Italy alone, not to mention Belgium and Holland, were enough to furnish a colony of museums and official residences. The looting was so systematic and pervasive that it took more than six years to identify and return the bulk of the booty, and efforts to identify and relocate further items, although delayed by the Cold War, continue to this day, especially in Germany and Russia where there remain—or appear to remain—many hidden treasures.

The recovery of stolen art as well as the repair and restoration of partially or totally destroyed architectural monuments has been a daunting task. The American museum establishment led by Paul Sachs, the legendary director of the Fogg Art Museum, and his influential colleague, the conservator George Stout, pleaded with the United States military authorities to include a group of trained specialists among their forces. Called Monuments, Fine Art, and Archives (MFAA) officers, the members of this group—many of them idealistic young students of art and history (at that time the history of art as a discipline had existed in America for no more than a generation)—later assumed positions of leadership in the post-war expansion of American museums. They included the Metropolitan Museum's James Rorimer and Ted Rousseau; Baltimore's and later Washington's Chuck Parkhurst; the Modern's and later Yale's Andrew Ritchie; and San Francisco's Thomas Howe as well as Harvard's Sachs and Stout. Some of this country's most prominent post-war educators and scholars also served in the MFAA. Craig Hugh Smyth, director of the Institute of Fine Arts of New York University and later director of Harvard's Villa I Tatti, had a leading role as did Sumner Crosby of Yale, Frederick Hartt of Virginia, Charles Sawyer of Michigan, and Lane Faison of Williams—the latter the father to a virtual generation of curatorial talent (Kirk Varnedoe, Jim Wood, Jack Lane, and Rusty Powell, among others). Safeguarding Europe's cultural patrimony in a time of great peril was an experience that fostered an understanding of the special responsibility of an art museum to cultivate the appreciation of art as an undertaking of great significance.

The words of Franklin Roosevelt on the occasion of the inauguration of the National Gallery of Art in Washington in 1941 echo this sentiment. On behalf of a democratic nation, President Roosevelt accepted the private donation of paintings from Andrew Mellon and others as not only works of art but also as symbols of the sort of world that freedom of the human spirit made possible and that now seemed so endangered by conflicts abroad. In accepting the art for the nation, Roosevelt reaffirmed the country's commitment to fight for such values. No better argument could have been made for art's importance to a young country with relatively little history and culture of its own. His prophetic statement became a rallying cry for museums in America to encourage a mutual understanding among diverse people through art and culture.

EDMUND P. PILLSBURY, PH.D.

DIRECTOR, KIMBELL ART MUSEUM (1980-1998)

AUTHOR'S PREFACE

Fascination with World War II and the absolute evil of Hitler and the Nazis seems endless. It is difficult to imagine any aspect of this enormous story that has not been exhaustively presented to the broader public. Yet how many among us know that Hitler saw himself as a talented artist who, as an eighteen year old, applied for admission to the Academy of Fine Arts in Vienna only to be rejected by a group of jurors, several of whom were Jewish?

For the remaining thirty-eight years of his life Adolf Hitler would continue to see himself as an artist and architect, a creator, with an unyielding determination to prove to the world his genius. All the while his anti-Semitism would grow in strength seeking outlets, first in his writing and speeches, and ultimately through the devastating actions of the Nazi party. The power of humiliation, rejection, and revenge were never more lethally combined.

Hitler and the Nazis established the most thorough and extensive looting operation in history, particularly the theft of art and other cultural objects. Their actions parallel similar episodes in stories of earlier conquerors. What sets this story apart from other such historical events was the response of America and her Allies. Their determination to prosecute a war while minimizing damage to cultural monuments and art works, and later recovering stolen objects for return to their rightful owners, was extraordinary.

In 1941, confronting a prolonged and truly world war unlike mankind had ever seen, President Roosevelt publicly committed the United States to the protection of Europe's cultural treasures when he stated:

. . . the purpose of the people of America [is] that the freedom of the human spirit and human mind which has produced the world's great art and all its science—shall not be utterly destroyed.

Imagine our world today had America not taken this lead role. Imagine a world where mankind's artistic legacy was moved about on an unprecedented scale, where whole sections of collections in public museums were removed on a whim and sold or destroyed. Imagine a world with no *Mona Lisa* or *The Last Supper*. Visitors to the Czartoryski Museum in Cracow need not imagine, for they have too often stared at an empty frame wondering if the missing painting by Raphael will ever reappear.

The passage of time can lead to forgetting painful and costly lessons paid for by our parents and grandparents. A friend once said, "Everything we know and learn in our lifetime will change except history." The rate of change today is relentless. We face an ever increasing risk of being too busy to heed and, as a result, blinded to the lessons.

Leonardo da Vinci,
The Last Supper, **1495-98.**
Fresco, 4.2 × 9.1 m (13 ft 9 in × 29 ft 10 in).
Refectory, Santa Maria delle Grazie, Milan.

"All things beautiful and mortal pass,
but not art."

LEONARDO DA VINCI

Protecting *The Last Supper*

The Last Supper, painted on the wall of the refectory (dining hall) in Santa Maria delle Grazie, was braced with metal rods and sandbags. In the final stage of protection, the fresco was completely boarded up to shield it from bombing and vibration.
Milan

An errant Allied bomb landed in the courtyard of Santa Maria delle Grazie. Three of the four structural walls were destroyed; one survived due only to the protective measures taken by local art officials.
August 1943

Major-General Willis D. Crittemberg and Field Marshall Alexander made a point of visiting Milan to see *The Last Supper*—after its miraculous survival of the bombings in August 1943—and, of course, to enjoy its wondrous glory.

During World War II America's military leadership learned from mistakes such as the decision to destroy the historic Abbey of Monte Cassino. Although the Allies eventually won the battle, it was a public relations debacle in the experienced hands of the masters of propaganda, Nazi Germany. The lesson of that experience was clear: a nation's leaders must be sensitive to and aware of the cultural treasures of others. Creation of the Monuments, Fine Arts, and Archives (MFAA) section and the work of the Monuments Men largely achieved that. After the battle of Monte Cassino, damage to cultural monuments still occurred, but it was gradually seen as an unavoidable consequence of winning the war.

The controversy surrounding the looting of the Iraq Museum in Baghdad in April, 2003, wasn't about how many objects were stolen which, in the end, was just six percent of the original estimate; rather, it concerned a lack of sensitivity and preparedness in anticipating such problems and accusations. Already, a lesson from World War II had been lost.

Explaining why art matters, why efforts to save a cultural treasure are worth the risk of a human life, is not easy. Yet history has provided us with the best answer. The cultural heritage of the world belongs to the future. Our future is diminished without them. These "things" have already survived centuries filled with conflict and destruction because others before us knew this too. Their survival was anything but an accident.

During World War II the actions of American and Allied military leaders, servicemen and women, in particular a group of young art history professionals, museum directors and personnel who constituted the MFAA section, demonstrated that art and culture matter greatly. GIs affirmed this with their careful work in the war zones, their attendance at art exhibitions set up by MFAA officers, and by their visits—for so many their first—to Europe's great cultural monuments as time and circumstance permitted. Is it a coincidence that the cultural arts in the United States—painting, film, music, dance, architecture—flourished after World War II, only a few years after the return of millions of American servicemen and women from their tours of duty in Europe?

One of the joys of following your heart is not knowing where it will lead, yet having a sense of purpose along the way. It has been quite a personal journey since reading Lynn Nicholas's book in June, 1996. This project became a labor of love for me. It consumed my life these past two years, pushing me to learn new skills and grow in so many areas. The writing was an exceedingly lonely challenge made all the more difficult by the sudden loss of two people I so dearly loved. From one I drew courage and reassurance; the other took a fairly empty page and filled it with love and happiness.

A book of this magnitude is the result of a team effort. Lynn

Nicholas was encouraging and helpful from the first day we met. Her guidance along the way contributed greatly. Ted Pillsbury made several introductions to museum colleagues and provided me with his perspective on this important period. My assistant and project coordinator, Karen Evans, embraced this project from the outset with the same degree of passion I felt. Her loyalty and commitment to excellence have been exemplary. My curator and art researcher, Shelley Matthews, is a testament to the quality of art history students being graduated from universities today. She has contacted archives throughout the Western world in search of photographs and information for this book. Our team of researchers—Sophie Richard, Andrzej Lewandowski, Sabine Ranft, Sim Smiley, Tamara Hufschmidt and Sergei Beck are the best; they always came through. This book is filled with examples of their dogged pursuit. My colleagues at Actual Films, Bonni Cohen, Jon Shenk, Nicole Newnham —in particular, Richard Berge—have been of invaluable assistance in helping us find critically important photographs. My editor and designer, Joshua Weikersheimer (with his file and layout master, Erik Tanck), have my eternal thanks and appreciation. Mark Suroff was kind enough to arrange the introduction.

Dozens of others working in archive facilities and universities in the United States, Europe, and Russia helped us, repeatedly. Of special note were Lauren Melo, Anne Ritchie, Jean Henry, and the rest of the Gallery Archives staff at the National Gallery of Art in Washington who graciously and patiently accommodated our visits, research and publication needs, as well as Meg Melvin of the Library Image Collections who contributed her expert knowledge of Munich Collecting Point materials; John Taylor of the Modern Military Branch of the National Archives and Records Administration, who was always available for any inquiry or request we made, and to fellow staff members, Holly Reed and Rutha Beaman of the Still Pictures Department; Linda Seckeleson and Robyn Fleming of the Thomas J. Watson Library at the Metropolitan Museum of Art; Gabrielle St. John-McAlister and Margaret Daly of the National Gallery in London; and finally, Cesi Kellinger, who so resourcefully hunted down every out of print book and catalogue we needed. They understood the importance of our project and made it theirs. I appreciate all that each of you did to put our requests at the front of the line.

To my family, friends, and supporters, thank you for believing in me and my ability to complete a project of this magnitude. In particular, Tom, June, and Mike: your constant support and willingness to listen sustained me. Finally, to my beloved son Diego, thank you for being so understanding of my deadlines during the precious few days we have together.

Venice
Allied servicemen and women in Piazza San Marco after liberation.

"Time and again during the two and a half centuries of our national existence, our political and intellectual leaders as well as our Average American have crossed the seas to make intimate, firsthand contacts with the surviving evidences of past cultures and to draw renewed inspiration therefrom. No amount of book knowledge by itself can equal the experience of actual contact or association."

LT. COL. ERNEST T. DEWALD
MONUMENTS, FINE ARTS, AND ARCHIVES OFFICER

RESCUING DA VINCI

For the Monuments Men who rescued it,
for my parents, Norma and Ray, who provided me with the opportunity to see it,
and for my son, Diego, who lives in its midst, to whom I leave this legacy.

PROLOGUE

During the course of World War II, Hitler and the Nazis planned and executed thefts of an unprecendented magnitude. While Hitler's focus remained on stealing the greatest artworks of Western European civilization, the Nazi machinery organized and implemented thefts of almost every item imaginable: from paintings, sculpture, porcelain, furniture, rugs, and tapestries, to gold, diamonds, currency, and jewelry, plus stained glass, church bells, entire libraries, and street cars, to military and religious artifacts, musical instruments and wine. Early success was intoxicating and, in time, everything seemed obtainable. For the Führer, no desired object was too large or important to steal, especially when it provided an opportunity to correct the wrongs of history and humiliate those responsible.

It is difficult to imagine that photographs of any single event could convey a story of such immensity while also providing a precise insight into the motives of its mastermind. However, the following photographs of the French surrender to Germany on June 22, 1940, do just that with startling clarity. With a keen sense of the past and an extraordinary understanding of the power of images, Hitler was determined to undo "the crime of Compiègne," the French town about fifty miles northeast of Paris where Germany surrendered to France on November 11, 1918, thereby concluding World War I. Ever the performance artist, Hitler located the Pullman railcar in which the German surrender of 1918 had taken place, had it removed from the nearby museum in Rethondes, then towed to the exact spot it had occupied twenty-two years earlier. The stage was then set for Hitler to rewrite history and, in so doing, humiliate the French just as he had been humiliated in his youth by the rejection of his life's ambition: recognition as an artist.

Compiègne, France
June 21, 1940

Standing in front of the historic railcar are the following (left to right):
Von Ribbentrop, Raeder, Brueckner, Hitler, Keitel, Göring, Von Brauchitsch, and Hess.

November 11, 1918
Marshal Foch (second from right) and others pose in front of the railcar in which they signed the armistice agreement with Germany that formally ended World War I.

Almost 22 years later, German officers examine the stone monument to World War I hero Marshal Foch as the railcar is towed into position after removal from the nearby museum at Rethondes, where it had been on display.

Hitler in the Armchair
Hitler sat in the same armchair used by Marshal Foch years earlier and faced the French representatives General Huntzinger and Vice-Admiral Le Luc, but only long enough to hear the reading of the preamble by General Keitel (standing to Hitler's left). Negotiations would continue until June 22 at 6:50 pm.

"*I observed his face. It was grave, solemn, yet brimming with revenge. There was also in it, as in his springy step, a note of the triumphant conqueror, the defier of the world. There was something else, difficult to describe, in his expression, a sort of scornful inner joy at being present at this great reversal of fate—a reversal he himself had wrought.*"

WILLIAM SHIRER
BERLIN DIARY

Berlin

After the surrender ceremony, the railcar was taken
to Berlin where it was towed down Unter den Linden
to the Lustgarten on the banks of the River Spree,
which at the time was frequently used for Nazi
parades and rallies. There it became a popular tourist
site. With increasing damage to Berlin from Allied
bombing, the Waffen SS moved the railcar to
Thuringia where it was subsequently destroyed by fire.
March 1941

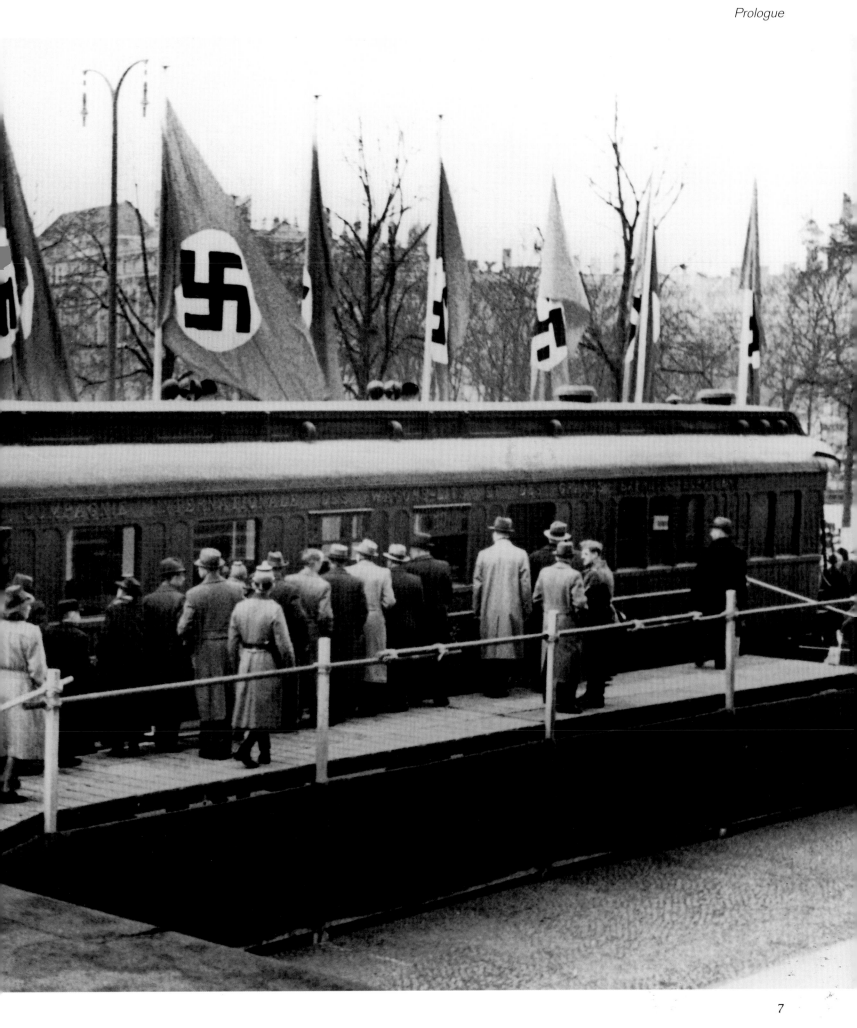

SETTING THE STAGE

CHAPTER 1

"Propaganda must not serve the truth especially insofar as it might bring out something favorable for the opponent."

"The crowd will finally succeed in remembering only the simplest concepts repeated a thousand times."

"We call upon our artists to wield the noblest weapon in the defense of the German people: German Art!"

ADOLF HITLER

"The Führer loves art because he himself is an artist. Under his blessed hand a Renaissance has begun."

JOSEPH GOEBBELS, REICHSMINISTER FOR PROPAGANDA AND NATIONAL ENLIGHTENMENT

"To whom should propaganda be addressed? To the scientifically trained intelligentsia or to the less educated masses? It must be addressed always and exclusively to the masses....The art of propaganda lies in understanding the emotional ideas of the great masses and finding...the way to the attention and thence to the heart of the broad masses."
ADOLF HITLER

Words seem inadequate to bring to life the evil incarnate and wanton destruction caused by the leadership of Adolf Hitler. There are innumerable villains in this story, but the goals of totalitarian domination of the world and racial supremacy originated in but one. For more than thirteen years his ideas, visions, and words pervaded a nation of 68 million people. Hitler's projections to the German people proved as hollow as they were fateful. In the end, what remained was a man whose sole ambition was power: power to control, power to create, and ultimately power to destroy. For a time his success was unparalleled.

Paradoxically, Hitler saw himself as an artist, no doubt the result of his early aspirations as a painter. In his words:

...One day it became clear to me that I would become a painter, an artist ... My father was struck speechless.... 'Artist! No! Never as long as I live!' ... My father would never depart from his 'Never!' and I intensified my 'Nevertheless!'

9

This was not destined to be his path, however. His examination results at Vienna's Academy of Fine Arts in 1907 were deemed inadequate by the jurors, several of whom were Jewish. Two other Austrians applying to art schools at about the same time were accepted: Egon Schiele and Oskar Kokoschka. Both would, in time, become leaders of the modern art movement, their work ridiculed by Hitler. Although encouraged by the Academy's Director to pursue architecture, Hitler was denied admittance to retake the exam upon applying the following year. His rejection was a bitter blow marking the low point of his young life. Despite this disappointment, Hitler created several thousand drawings, watercolors, and oil paintings. More prophetically, he drew numerous detailed sketches of urban planning and building designs. Years later, he drew plans for a museum complex he envisioned for Linz, Austria, his hometown. The idea of the "Führer Museum" was perhaps born out of the humiliation of his rejection as an artist. It would consume his life until the bitter end.

After moving to Germany, a country he admired, and serving in a Bavarian regiment of the German Army during World War I, Hitler settled in Munich. His creative energies now sought a new outlet: politics. The ensuing years of stagflation followed by the worldwide depression of 1929 provided fertile ground and eager followers—especially among the approximately six million unemployed Germans. What was needed? Someone to deliver a message that directed blame to others, mainly Jews, and promised a brighter future. Now Germany could ascend to its rightful leadership role in Europe and beyond. It was the setting for a "perfect storm," which would create the void Hitler masterfully filled.

Nuremberg became the nexus of Nazi party rallies beginning in 1933, the year Hitler became Chancellor of Germany. For one week each September, these rallies were attended by hundreds of thousands of people, from lowest wage workers to Nazi party officials. The pageantry and stage designs by Nazi architect Albert Speer were astonishing. In the course of the week, parades, bands, torchlight ceremonies, and a sea of flags and banners prevailed; night skies were illuminated with searchlights which provided the dramatic backdrop for the endless speeches that preceded Hitler's closing remarks.

Leaving nothing to chance, Hitler and other Nazi party officials commissioned acclaimed actress and director Leni Riefenstahl to produce two films, documentary in nature, of the Nuremberg Rallies of September, 1933 and 1934. Marked by keen cinematic artistry, her 1934 film entitled *Triumph of the Will* is considered by many to be the greatest propaganda film ever produced. With masterful direction, Ms. Riefenstahl relentlessly depicted the

Nazi party as strong and unified. The rallies, speeches, and films succeeded in their message by whipping those in attendance into an emotional frenzy, then returning them as "disciples" to their communities to spread their fanaticism to others.

In building power, few weapons in Hitler's arsenal were used with greater long-term effect than that of art and architecture. Hitler defined and dictated the standards. That which didn't measure up to his definition and taste simply wasn't art. Over and over again, he repeated this message—at rallies, dedication ceremonies, and the Reich party Congress. In Hitler's view, "modern" art—the work of such artists as Pablo Picasso, Henri Matisse, Wassily Kandinsky, Marc Chagall, Amedeo Modigliani, Piet Mondrian, Max Beckmann, and fellow Austrians Oscar Kokoschka and Egon Schiele, to name only a few—was "degenerate." Such art destroyed the classical concept of beauty and replaced it with interpretive works that were incomprehensible to the viewer. As a group, the "degenerates" included immigrants, foreigners, and Jews, all of whom Hitler deemed racially inferior. Hitler made certain to link their work with that of intellectuals, the elites of society who had social agendas. According to Hitler, these were the people responsible for Germany's post-World War I problems and who bore the blame for its decline. Even late nineteenth-century artists such as Vincent van Gogh, Paul Gauguin, and Edgar Degas were included among these reviled painters, for in Hitler's view, the distorted figures and bold colors of their work could only be the product of sick minds.

In contrast, German Art—true art—was "of the people" and expressed the moral values of the Third Reich. It was easy to comprehend, often depicting scenes of everyday life or landscapes. Artistic renderings of the human form, following the classical models of ancient Greece, further embodied Hitler's concept of the eternal value of beauty. His favorite sculptors, Josef Thorak and Arno Breker, created dramatic oversized pieces portraying semi-clad male and female figures in poses that idealized youth, strength, heroism, and sacrifice.

Hitler also admired nineteenth-century painters such as Ferdinand Georg Waldmüller, Franz von Lenbach, and Wilhelm Liebl. In his view, these artists' work promoted strength of family and the unity of the German people. These attributes would be greatly needed in the coming years. Old Master painters such as Jan Vermeer, Rembrandt van Rijn, Leonardo da Vinci, and Jan van Eyck, along with the great German artists Lucas Cranach and Hans Holbein, had stood the test of time and were universally recognized as the epitome of greatness. Hitler believed ownership of such icons would bring recognition of his sophisticated knowledge of art and refined taste.

Repatriation was another reason that Hitler coveted certain works. The repatriation argument was elucidated in the Kümmel Report, a 319-page document compiled by Dr. Otto Kümmel, Director of the Berlin Museums, at the behest of Hitler and later Goebbels. This report listed every artwork lost in war and removed from Germany during the previous 400 years and identified the precise location and owner of each piece. Kümmel distinguished those works considered to be by "historically significant artists" from those by "lesser" artists of only "local" importance. The report contained works located in all Western European countries in addition to Russia and even the United States. Virtually every form of art was addressed, making the report a "shopping list" that enabled Nazi officials to "reclaim" designated works from individuals, museums, and churches throughout the areas they occupied. In most instances, the basis for repatriation was specious. For example, an altarpiece created by the fifteenth-century artist Veit Stoss, a native of Nuremberg, was removed by the Nazis from Cracow and taken to Nuremberg solely on the basis that Veit Stoss was German-born.

Art as propaganda encompassed more than pictures, film, and words alone. In the summer of 1937, new methods were implemented that would have far-reaching consequences. Munich was the site of two events that were designed to leave no doubt in the minds of the people about the difference between "good" art and that which was unacceptable. On July 18 the four-month-long show entitled "Great German Art Exhibition," opened at the newly completed House of German Art, the first Nazi public building project. Hitler had participated in the selection of works for the show. Opening ceremonies included a parade and other festivities that culminated in a speech in which the Führer derided modern art and artists, gallery owners and art critics, among others. This exhibition would become an annual event in which Hitler's enthusiastic participation was assured.

Opening the following day was a show entitled "Degenerate Art" (*Entartete Kunst*), also "curated" in part by Hitler. Here, rather than glorifying the artists and their works as was being done at the German Art Exhibition, every possible effort was made to degrade and humiliate them. Paintings were juxtaposed in a manner unseen previously; some hung crooked, others were positioned above doorways or clumped together to create the most negative visual effect. Large panels were hung throughout the exhibition containing quotations by Hitler and Goebbels ridiculing and condemning the works. Purchase prices were often cited in an attempt to show how the public had been duped. These efforts were designed to convince the viewing public of the insidious nature of these "perverted" artists and their work. Every effort was made to instill in the visitors the same sense of revulsion so emphatically pronounced by the Führer. In contrast to the 400,000 people who visited the House of German Art Exhibition, more than 2,000,000 people attended the "Degenerate Art" exhibition in Munich. The show subsequently was sent to cities throughout Germany to spread and repeat the propaganda.

The "degenerate" artworks included in the exhibition had come from the most unlikely of places: museums throughout Germany. In 1937 Goebbels had organized a committee which was ordered to seize such artwork from the State Museums. More than 16,000 works of modern art—including masterpieces of the highest quality—were removed from these institutions' walls and stored in Berlin. Selections of the most "disgusting" works were readied for inclusion in the "Degenerate Art" Exhibition.

In 1938 Reichsmarshall Hermann Göring suggested selling the seized "degenerate" art to raise foreign currency. This idea was embraced by the Führer who had previously visited the warehouses containing many of these works. Goebbels now created The Commission for the Disposal of Products of Degenerate Art, whose members included Heinrich Hoffmann, Hitler's personal photographer, and Karl Haberstock, a noted Berlin art dealer who had already sold many works of art to the Führer. The Commission was charged with determining the best method to sell the selected pieces. In late 1938 a decision was made to send 126 "degenerate" works to Galerie Fischer in Lucerne, Switzerland, for public auction. Considerable controversy arose prior to the sale due to public perception that the proceeds would be used by the German government for the purchase of armaments. To quell such talk, Theodore Fischer made public statements that sales proceeds would in fact be used by German museums to fund new art acquisitions, a preposterous notion given the irreplaceable nature of the works being sold.

The Galerie Fischer sale took place on June 30, 1939, at the Grand Hotel National and was attended by approximately 350 people. Of the 126 items listed, almost eighty percent were sold for a modest sum of only $115,000. The star lot, Van Gogh's *Self Portrait*, which had been confiscated from the Neue Staatsgalerie in Munich, sold for about $40,000 to a private New York collector. Several other works were also acquired by American collectors. European museums such as the Kunstmuseum in Basel, Switzerland, and a group of museums in Belgium including the Musée des Beaux-Arts in Liège, made opportune additions to their existing collections.

Overall, however, the disappointing results discouraged further public sales. A small group of German dealers did subsequently sell various works privately but the prices were usually ridiculously low. Many unsold confiscated works including those removed from German museums were eventually destroyed. More than 4,000 works of art were tossed into a bonfire in 1939 as part of a fire department training exercise.

As the newly appointed Chancellor, Hitler made state visits to Venice in 1934, and to Florence and Rome in 1938 and 1940. No doubt these trips further stoked his artistic ambitions. The pageantry of the Third Reich already owed much to the great civilization of Rome. Hitler's taste in art embraced the epic stature of the male model of antiquity. Upon his arrival in Florence the Führer had the opportunity to see the extraordinary achievements of artists who worked in Florence during the Renaissance, including a four-hour visit to the Uffizi Gallery with Italian Dictator Benito Mussolini. Having seen those artworks many times before, Mussolini was heard to mutter, probably out of boredom, *"Tutti questi quadri… [All these pictures…]."* "He [Hitler] never stopped expressing his joy that the visits to Rome and Florence had made it possible to admire immortal masterpieces that he had previously known only from photographs." These visits confirmed for Hitler that existing collections in German museums did not possess all the great works he would need for the Führer Museum.

By late 1937, Hilter had assembled a modest collection of mediocre works or art. Germany's annexation of Austria in March, 1938, would radically alter matters by creating the opportunity to plunder established world-class collections. A year later, Hitler appointed the distinguished director of the Dresden Gemäldegalerie, Dr. Hans Posse, to make additional acquisitions for his collection and future museum. More importantly, Posse had the right of first refusal on all confiscated artworks which he would utilize to select the pieces of highest quality for the Linz Collection. Posse had other advantages, not the least of which was unrestricted access to Hitler via his assistant, Martin Bormann. He had almost limitless funds at his disposal and a large staff to handle the acquisition activity and subsequent shipping of artworks. By December, 1944, the funds appropriated for Linz were a staggering $28 million dollars ($312,480,000 in 2005 dollars).

Whether Hitler's objective for Linz was to build the world's greatest museum, largest museum, or a museum of the greatest quality is a question that continues to be exhaustively studied. There is no debate, however, that those objects not destined for the Führer Museum—out of the estimated 5,000 to 8,000 artworks that were confiscated, stolen, or acquired by threat—were to be distributed to satellite museums throughout the Third Reich. Hitler was determined to diminish Vienna's cultural preeminence while elevating Linz to the cultural capital of Europe. Hitler's rejection—in his eyes, humiliation—by the Academy of Fine Arts in Vienna would now be

"repaid" in many ways. Although his museum was never built, its plans and architectural models were a constant focus of the Führer, even during the final desperate days in the Berlin bunker.

Others in the Nazi hierarchy also possessed ambition to collect great works of art. Göring was driven by his passion for art. His appetite was insatiable. Given his favored status with Hitler in the early years of the war, and his control over transportation by train and plane as head of the Air Force, Göring had critical resources which he used vigorously to add to his collections. Considering himself "the last Renaissance man," Göring certainly had a more cultivated sense of taste than Hitler which he amply demonstrated at his country estate, Carinhall, located about fifty miles from Berlin. Like Hitler, he also had an advisor for acquisitions; Walter Andreas Hofer. Ironically, Göring would, in time, find himself in competition with Hitler for the very best paintings.

In contrast, Goebbels, Heinrich Himmler (SS Reichsführer and Gestapo Chief), Hans Frank (Governor-General of Nazi-occupied Poland), Alfred Rosenberg (head of the special unit, Einsatzstab Reichsleiter Rosenberg known as the "ERR," which plundered objects of art and furniture belonging to Jews in occupied Europe), Kajetan Mühlmann (Special Commissioner for the Safekeeping of Works of Art in the Occupied Territories and special purchaser for Göring in Berlin, Vienna, and Warsaw), along with countless other Nazi officials for the most part played "follow the leader," eager to please their Führer and show their loyalty by participating in the looting of Europe. Methodically, systematically, continually, individuals, museums, and churches were "relieved" of their precious belongings. It would continue for seven long years.

"The broad mass of a people… falls victim to a big lie more easily than to a small one."
ADOLF HITLER

Nuremberg Rally
September 1935
The annual September rallies in Nuremberg were "masterpieces of theatrical art."
"I had spent six years in St. Petersburg before the war in the best days of the old Russian ballet," wrote British Ambassador Sir Nevile Henderson, "but for grandiose beauty I have never seen a ballet to compare with it."

"In the evening the people's will power more easily succumbs . . .

. . . to the dominating force of a stronger will."   JOSEPH GOEBBELS

"But the masses are slow moving, and they always require a certain time before they are ready even to notice a thing, and only after the simplest ideas are repeated thousands of times will the masses finally remember them...."

ADOLF HITLER

PREVIOUS PAGE

"Cathedral of Light"

Albert Speer, Hitler's personal architect, had the idea to conduct one of the party rallies at night using 130 flak searchlights, almost the entire reserve of Luftwaffe. "If we use them in such large numbers for a thing like this, other countries will think we're swimming in searchlights," commented Hitler.

"The actual effect far surpassed anything I had imagined. The 130 sharply defined beams, placed around the field at intervals of 40 feet, were visible to a height of 25,000, after which they merged into a general glow. The feeling was of a vast room, with the beams serving as mighty pillars of infinitely high outer walls.... I imagined that this 'cathedral of light' was the first luminescent architecture...."

ALBERT SPEER, HITLER'S PERSONAL ARCHITECT

Kristallnacht (Crystal Night)

Nazi leaders capitalized on the murder of a German official by a Jewish refugee to incite other Germans to take to the streets and vent their anger towards Jews and Jewish establishments. For two days Nazi gangs roamed the streets of cities throughout Germany. Broken glass littered streets hence the name *Kristallnacht*. In all, almost 200 synagogues were desecrated and more than 7,000 stores and businesses were looted.

November 9 and 10, 1938

"...And then, to our amazement, we shall see what tremendous results such perseverence leads to,... results that are almost beyond our understanding."

Adolf Hitler

ART AS PROPAGANDA

KUNST DEM VOLK

WEHRMACHTSAUSGABE

HERAUSGEBER: PROF. HEINRICH HOFFMANN

A Cover of *Kunst dem Volk*
"Art of the People," a Nazi journal, which displayed a painting of German soldiers on its front cover. The journal was edited by Hitler's personal photographer, Heinrich Hoffmann, who wrote in another edition, "As our leader saved the German people from the threatening chaos of Bolshevism, so he also protected the German soul ... and especially German art from degeneration.... German art is again healthy."

" 'Works of art' that are not capable of being understood in themselves but need some pretentious instruction book to justify their existence—until at long last they find someone sufficiently browbeaten to endure such stupid or impudent twaddle with patience—will never again find their way to the German people."

ADOLF HITLER

Munich

This statement was part of the remarks made by Hitler at the opening of the House of German Art. As part of the ceremony there was an elaborate parade through Königsplatz.
July 1937

Hitler the Curator

Hitler was integrally involved in the planning and curating of the Great German Art exhibitions held each July from 1937-1943 at the House of German Art in Munich. Items in the exhibition were for sale, but most were purchased by the government as the artwork had little popular appeal.

July 1937

Berlin

By order of the Führer, more than 16,000 modern works deemed "degenerate" were removed from the walls of German museums. By 1937 works by artists such as Nolde, Kandinsky, Klee, Dix, Chagall, Kokoschka, Beckmann and many others were collecting dust in various storage facilities pending their new fate. Hitler, accompanied by Goebbels, was seemingly always available when an opportunity arose to see art, especially when it could be used for such effective propaganda purposes.
January 1938

"Degenerate Art"

Crowds of people including Nazi officials lined up to see the "Degenerate Art" Exhibition at the House of Art (*Haus der Kunst*) in Berlin. Goebbels, Hitler and other Nazi officials visited the show in Munich in 1937. A view of one wall with works of art by Baum, Belling, Campendonk, Dexel, Felixmüller, Hoffmann, Feininger, Nolde, and Margarethe Moll.

Hitler Visits the "Exhibition of Disgrace"
The painting is Erich Heckel's *Seated Man*, which
was acquired by the Stadtmuseum Dresden in
1920. After appearing here it was seized and
shown at the "Degenerate Art" exhibition in
Munich in 1937. It has not been seen since.
Dresden, August 1935

25

Museum Collections: Sold!

In 1939, 126 post-Impressionist and modern pictures were placed with the Fischer Gallery in Lucerne for auction. These works were considered "degenerate" and had been among the thousands removed from German museums by order of Hitler and Goebbels. The result of the sale was a disappointment; proceeds totaled a mere $115,000. The Van Gogh *Self Portrait,* removed from the Neue Staatsgalerie in Munich, was Germany's loss but America's gain. It now hangs in the Fogg Museum at Harvard, having been purchased by Mr. Maurice Wertheim who subsequently donated it to the museum. The Picasso *Head of a Woman*, which had been removed from the Städtische Galerie, Frankfurt, sold for only $1,800 to an absentee bidder named "M. Dietz." It reappeared at public auction in 2001 and sold to an undisclosed buyer for $6.8 million.

"Paintings from the degenerate art auction will now be offered on the international art market. In so doing we hope at least to make some money from this garbage."

JOSEPH GOEBBELS

Hitler the Artist

These two watercolors, owned by Heinrich Hoffmann, were seized by soldiers of the U.S. Army. Hitler painted the one above in 1914. The other was painted in 1917 after he had been gassed during battle in World War I. Both paintings are now in the National Museum of the U.S. Army, Army Art Collection, Washington, D.C.

OPPOSITE

Hitler sketching architectural ideas for the Linz Museum.

THE DREAM OF LINZ

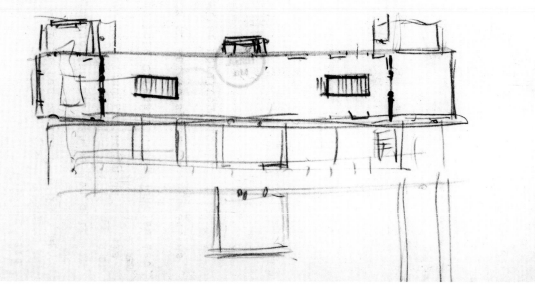

Zeichnung des Führers, Nacht v.12./13.5.42 im Führerhaupt-
quartier bei Rastenburg.

Grundriss der neuen Linzer Galerie.

Hitler the Architect

Hitler detested Vienna and its high society. He intended to exact revenge for his rejection as an aspiring artist by diminishing Vienna's cultural dominance of Austria through the rebuilding on the most dramatic and lavish scale of his hometown of Linz. Hitler made numerous sketches for the new museum he planned on building – The Führer Museum. By late 1942, these sketches had evolved into a scale model of what Linz would become.

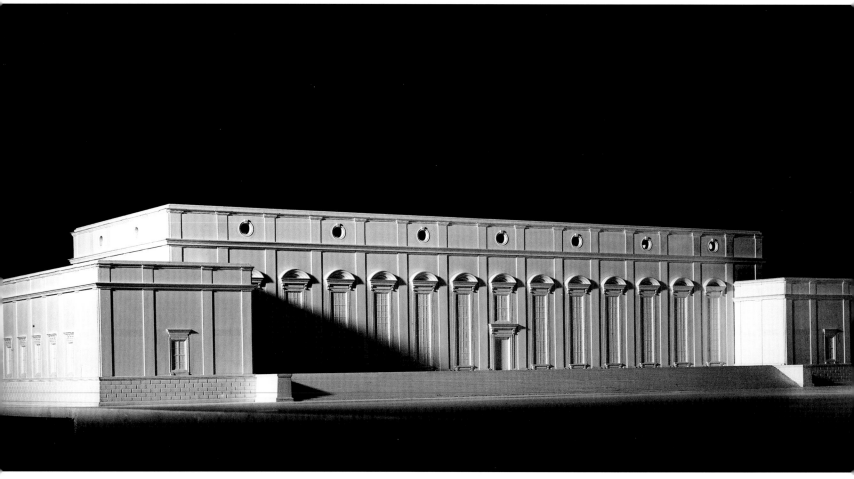

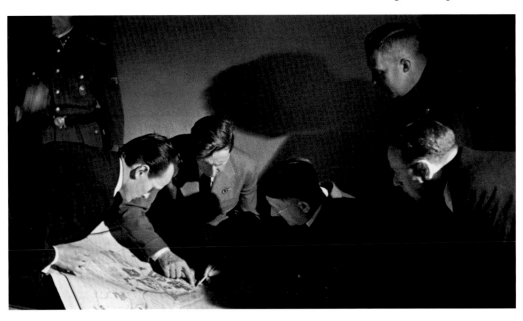

The "New" Linz

The Führer, sketch pencil in hand, intensely examines blueprints for the "new" Linz while those in attendance observe. In the middle photograph, resting on the arms of the conference room chairs, is a detailed drawing of the new city. In the photograph below, Hitler points to the scale model of Linz.

Studio of architect Hermann Giesler, 1943

As if conducting an orchestra, Hitler's animated enthusiasm for rebuilding Linz and the new museum was ever-present.

Hitler the Master Planner

The rebuilding of Linz and the building of the collection for the new museum consumed time, energy and manpower he might have otherwise used to prosecute the war. The dream continued to occupy him to the bitter end.
SEE PAGES 38-39.

APPRAISING ITALY

Rome

Hitler, Goebbels, Himmler and others were given a tour by Italian dictator Benito Mussolini of the Borghese Gallery, where they stopped to admire the sculpture of *Pauline Borghese Bonaparte* by Antonio Canova. These were formative visits for the Führer as he continued to develop plans for the new museum in Linz and its contents.
May 1938

Florence
Cheering Florentines packed Piazza Signoria to see Hitler and Mussolini stand on the balcony of the Palazzo Vecchio during the Führer's state visit to Italy.
October 1940

Hitler's 50th Birthday

He would experience only six more. As paintings were one of the prized gifts among the Nazi leadership, his office in the Reichchancellery was filled with such gifts and other works of art. Heinrich Himmler, head of the Gestapo, presented a painting to the Führer as a birthday gift.

New Assignment

Dr. Hans Posse, Director of the famed Gemäldegalerie in Dresden, was directed by a letter from Hitler dated June 26, 1939, to supervise the construction of the Führer Museum in Linz. "Herewith I am commissioning *Herr Galeriedirektor* [Director of the Museum/Gallery] Dr. Hans Posse, to build the new art museum in Linz-Donau. All Party and governmental offices are obliged to support Dr. Posse with the completion of this order."
—A. Hitler
Berlin 1939

OBERSALZBERG, den 26. Juni 1939

ADOLF HITLER·

Ich beauftrage Herrn Galeriedirektor Dr. Hans Posse, Dresden, mit dem Aufbau des neuen Kunstmuseums für die Stadt Linz/Donau.

Alle Partei- und Staatsdienststellen sind verpflichtet, Herrn Dr. Posse bei Erfüllung seiner Aufgabe zu unterstützen.

Seat of Power

A color photograph of Hitler's study in the new Reichschancellery, designed by Albert Speer. The room was 27.4 × 15.2 × 10.1 m (90 × 50 × 33 ft). It was an imposing and intimidating space designed to project the Führer's power and control.
Berlin 1939

An Imaginary Escape
With Giesler, Ordinance Officer Linge and Chief of
SS Intelligence Dr. Kaltenbrunner at his side, Hitler,
seemingly oblivious to the dire circumstances
outside the Führer bunker, enthusiastically gestures
at the model of Linz while explaining his dramatic
plans for the city.
March 1945

Obsessed to the End

With his enemies closing in on all sides, and only weeks away from suicide, Hitler stares at the model of Linz just as he had years earlier, perhaps contemplating all that might have been.

March 1945

ART'S GREATEST THIEVES

Hitler and Göring
Since their relationship began in 1922, Göring was always the number two man. He knew how to play the supporting role well. Whether relaxing together at a hunting lodge, enjoying a parade during the "2000 years of German culture" festival, or jointly admiring a painting, Hitler and Göring were linked as the leaders of the Nazi party until April 20, 1945, Hitler's final birthday and the last time they would see each other.

"Plundering Thoroughly"
Göring considered himself a great collector and connoisseur, a "Renaissance man." He enjoyed art and, unlike Hitler, had a passion for the chase and ownership of the object. Each conquered country opened up new opportunities so vast that Göring needed assistance. Hitler had the guidance of Hans Posse; Göring had the services of Walter Andreas Hofer, his personal curator. Hofer is standing in front of two paintings, one attributed to the School of Leonardo, now in the Uffizi (left), and the other by Giampietrino, now in the Staatliche Museen in Kassel, Germany.

Göring examines the surface of a painting while Hofer watches. In the photograph below, Göring accompanied by Hans Frank (on the right with arms crossed) visits an art exhibition.

Carinhall

Named after his deceased wife Carin, Göring's country estate began as a glorified log-cabin, but grew to a proportion befitting its owner. Göring regularly hosted dignitaries and other guests at elaborate events, all of which provided him with an opportunity to display his art collection and other possessions.

Paintings in the vast gallery included masters of the highest order: Cranach, Palma Vecchio, Breughel and Rubens. In the next few years, Göring's voracious appetite for art would result in a dramatic increase in the size of his collection to approximately 1,700 paintings. Still, he wanted more.

PREPARATIONS

"It was in the face of this appalling prospect that we had been charged, for the first time in our history, with the securing of the national artistic inheritance. Whatever the threats which weighed on its inhabitants, France was above all to save the spiritual values which it held as an integral part of its heart and its culture. To put at shelter its works of art, its archives, its libraries, was indeed one of the first reflexes of defense of our country."

ROSE VALLAND, LOUVRE CURATOR AND FRENCH MUSEUM HEROINE, *LE FRONT DE L'ART*

"Bury them in caves or cellars, but not a picture shall leave these islands."

PRIME MINISTER SIR WINSTON CHURCHILL, TELEGRAM TO SIR KENNETH CLARK, DIRECTOR OF THE NATIONAL GALLERY, LONDON

A museum custodian of the Louvre stands forlornly in a room filled with empty frames, the paintings having already been removed for packing. Note the chalk inscription on the wall above his cap indicating the name of the painting which formerly hung in that spot. This scene was being repeated throughout Europe's greatest museums and galleries as war seemed imminent.

Those geographically closest to Germany saw early warning signs that were all too familiar. They had heard Hitler speak, witnessed the fervor of his followers, understood something of his ambitions. In many instances, museum directors and curators grasped the danger sooner than government leaders. Late in 1936 the Spanish Civil War served not just as a dramatic prelude to the coming events but also illustrated the new dangers posed to cultural monuments and artworks as a result of technological developments in warfare. This lesson was forcefully presented through the damage caused by aerial bombardment, especially from incendiary bombs. As a precaution, the collections of the Prado Museum in Madrid were taken down and stored on the ground floor as there was no basement storage.

In late October, 1936, bombing commenced about twenty-five miles northwest of Madrid at El Escorial, the majestic monastery and palace of King Philip II, which contained a treasure trove of great art works by El Greco, Rogier van der Weyden, and Diego Velázquez, among others. Subsequent bombing near the Prado shattered its windows and precipitated the loading of the most valuable portion of the collection, numbering around 300 paintings, onto an armored train destined for Valencia. Within a year, the paintings had to be moved again to a castle near Barcelona and then several more times within Spain before finally being transported to Geneva. There they were exhibited, from June to early September of 1939, at the Museum of Art and History.

The exhibition included 174 paintings; it was a once-in-a-lifetime event. Many of these works would never have traveled under normal circumstances. That so much of one country's artistic patrimony would be transported from place to place for three years, then exhibited in a foreign country en masse, provides us with the sense of crisis that gripped officials in Spain. Art luminaries such as Kenneth Clark and Bernard Berenson, and people throughout Europe, traveled to Geneva to see it. Many believed this might be the last major art exhibition to be held in Europe for a very long time. The show featured mostly works from the Prado in Madrid but also included a few from the Academy of San Fernando and El Escorial. Most notable among these were Van der Weyden's masterpiece, the *Deposition* (El Escorial), Velázquez's *Las Méninas* (Prado), and Albrecht Dürer's *Self Portrait* of 1498 (Prado). There were more than 26 paintings by El Greco, 38 by Goya, and 34 by Velázquez. It may well have been the single greatest art exhibition ever.

These developments convinced museum authorities in neighboring countries of the need to protect their valued objects and monuments. Although some perfunctory planning for evacuation and protection of collections had been initiated in the mid 1930s, it wasn't until 1937 that officials in Western Europe and the United Kingdom began preparing in earnest. The task local officials faced was colossal. Beginning with the formation of lists of only the most important and valued works, curators had to consider possible storage sites that would provide security for the objects that were accessible by truck or rail, then develop various evacuation routes. The sheer volume of items, the size and weight of others, and the shortages of personnel and protective materials (brick, mortar, lumber, transportation vehicles, etc.) that had to be overcome were staggering.

In the course of preparations, every conceivable method of protecting artworks was implemented. Objects that were too large or heavy to transport, such as Michelangelo's sculpture of *David*, were protected first by scaffolds and supporting sandbags, and finally by brick "entombment." Immovable objects, such as Leonardo da Vinci's fresco of *The Last Supper* in Milan, were braced with structural supports and faced with protective boards further weighted in place by sandbags. Huge canvases were taken out of their frames and off their wooden stretchers, then rolled like maps. Massive sculptures were disassembled when possible and hidden. Paintings were packed in crates, usually without their frames, and prepared for storage. Entire structures, such as the fourth-century Arch of Constantine in Rome, were encased with structural supports of wood, steel, sandbags, and brick. For the largest cultural monuments, such as Notre Dame in Paris, only certain sections of the church were protected, such as the carved stone areas above the entry. Stained glass windows, such as those in St. Chappelle in Paris and the Cathedral in Strasbourg, were removed. Fragile sculptures and pottery were often packed in sand. Ingenuity was at a premium.

Museums and churches evacuated their most priceless works of art to hundreds of repositories or hiding places. Frequently, when war did arrive, these artworks were loaded back onto vehicles—cars, trucks, even barges—and moved yet again. Individuals owning works of art had few options and far fewer resources. In several instances, wealthier collectors deposited their art in bank vaults or loaned them to museums for safekeeping. A few individuals were able to ship some or all of their collections to countries outside Europe. However, the great number of private collectors could only wait and hope that their worst fears would not be realized.

In England, preparations began in 1938 to establish repositories in the area of Wales which, at the time, seemed a safe distance from the threat of German bombing. Using the British Rail system, paintings from the National Gallery in London were first stored in various country homes and castles. However, with the fall of France in June, 1940, Germans were able to establish air bases that placed Wales (and the collections) in the path of bombing runs made on England's industrial cities. Circumstances had changed dramatically. As a result, officials sought an underground solution: Manod Quarry in Wales. Preparations to receive the collections required enlarged entrances, blasting rock to create additional storage space, and installation of a system to control light and humidity, all of which meant crates of paintings couldn't be received until August, 1941. Similar arrangements were made in nearby areas for artworks from the Victoria and Albert Museum, the British Museum, and the Tate Gallery. It was fortuitous: all these museums and the National Gallery were hit repeatedly and severely damaged by German bombs.

France and Holland did not have one obvious benefit of England: geographic location made them Germany's next door neighbors. As early as 1937, museum officials had compiled lists of "priority" items and identified churches and châteaux that could serve as storage facilities in case of evacuation. In 1938, under the supervision of the Director of the Louvre, Jacques Jaujard, custom designed crates were manufactured for the most important paintings. Upon the announcement of a German-Russian non-aggression pact on August 23, 1939, plans throughout Europe and the United Kingdom were urgently put into action. That day, the National Gallery in London announced its closing; the Rijksmuseum in Holland quickly followed. The Tate Gallery in London closed on August 24 with museums in Paris following suit on August 25. War was considered imminent. It was, in fact, less than a week away.

Germany's surprise attack on Poland on September 1, 1939, removed any remaining doubt of Hitler's intentions. By the time of Germany's invasion of France, Belgium, the Netherlands, and Luxembourg in May, 1940, officials were aware of the theft of historic works from Poland. No theft was more prominent than that of the remarkable altarpiece by Veit Stoss which Polish officials had removed from the Church of Our Lady in Cracow in an unsuccessful attempt to hide it from the Nazis. It became apparent that Germany had invested the same thoroughness of planning into the stealing of iconic cultural treasures as it had into the military operations of invasion. There were in fact "shopping lists" of items designated for priority "removal" and shipment to Germany. Museum officials everywhere thus went to extraordinary lengths to hide their masterpieces, such as Leonardo da Vinci's *Mona Lisa*, which for several years was on the move as the French were fearful of the painting's likely appeal to Hitler.

Events in these countries developed so quickly that private collectors and dealers had little or no time to safeguard their possessions. French collectors, in particular Jews, had hoped that by depositing their collections with those of major French museums, they would be out of the reach of the invading Germans. Unfortunately, German planners had identified the primary acquisition targets with precise information about who owned them and where they were located. It was only a matter of time—and threats—before the Germans would seize the hidden works.

Germany's attack on Russia on June 22, 1941, caught officials by surprise. There was virtually no time to protect the numerous country palaces and their innumerable treasures from the German army as it advanced on Leningrad (now St. Petersburg). The Winter Palace built by Catherine the Great, and Peterhof, among others, lay directly in their path. Officials at the great Hermitage Museum in Leningrad faced a task that would have been overwhelming in peacetime: protecting almost 2,000,000 art objects. They had long before made "priority" lists of their collections as had their counterparts in Western Europe. The most important items were immediately placed in the limited basement storage. Meanwhile, non-stop packing of the other valued pieces commenced. Of all the paintings in the Hermitage, only one received its own crate: Rembrandt's monumental *Return of the Prodigal Son*. Within twenty-four hours of Germany's invasion the first air raid on Leningrad occurred. Amazingly, by July 6, more than half a million art objects had been loaded onto twenty-two railcars in the museum's first train shipment to Siberia. Two weeks later a second train departed with 700,000 objects. Shortly thereafter, German forces severed the rail links. The German army was now just eight miles from the Hermitage. On September 4, 1941, the first artillery shells hit Leningrad; there would be no further evacuations.

In hindsight, it seems difficult to imagine that officials in Washington, D.C. could have been fearful of an attack that would have placed artworks in the National Gallery in harm's way, even after the December 7, 1941 surprise attack by Japan on Pearl Harbor. That officials at the newly opened museum did react in such a decisive manner so soon thereafter gives us a sense of the times. On New Year's Eve, 1941, 75 of the most important paintings were secretly removed from its walls, packed, and six days later shipped to the Biltmore Estate in Asheville, North Carolina, where they safely arrived the following week. There they would remain in protective custody for more than two years.

ENGLAND

Evacuation
National Gallery staff
evacuate a Renaissance
painting by the Venetian
artist Bonifazio di Pitati, in
late August, 1939.

London and Manod Quarry

Museum officials closed the National Gallery in London on August 23, 1939. Initially, paintings were evacuated and transported via the British Rail system to various castles and country homes in the area of Wales. As Germany stepped up its bombing runs targeting nearby industrial cities, museum officials moved the paintings again to an underground quarry at Manod, Wales. Paintings could not be received there until late summer 1941, due to the extensive preparation work required.
August 1939-1941

These photographs show the delivery and unloading of paintings inside the quarry. In the photograph at left, air-tight railway wagons filled with paintings are pushed into position for storage.

Between Penrhyn Castle and Manod Quarry
This vehicle, carrying a custom crate containing the
Van Dyck portrait of King Charles I, was in transit to
Manod for underground storage. Officials had to lower
the level of the road to create sufficient passage-way.
This was but one of many types of problems
confronting museum officials as they rushed to protect
their national heritage.

**Anthony van Dyck,
*Equestrian Portrait of
Charles I*, c. 1637-38.**
Oil on canvas, 3.7 × 2.9 m
(12 ft 2 in × 9 ft 6 in). The
National Gallery, London.

53

FRANCE

Greek, *Winged Victory of Samothrace*, 190 BCE.
Marble, H. 3.2 m (10 ft 9 in).
Louvre, Paris.

"The statue rocked onto an inclined wooden ramp, held back by two groups of men, who controlled her descent with ropes stretched to either side... the Victory rolled slowly forward, her stone wings trembling slightly."

Louvre Evacuation
In the photograph above, Louvre workers constructed a pulley to position the statue before crating it for shipment.
September 1939

A Louvre official maintains quiet watch in front of the space that once housed the great *Winged Victory of Samothrace*.

Many of the large paintings in the Louvre were rolled and then crated for shipment. However, the condition of some paintings was too fragile to store in this manner. This painting by Géricault was so large—4.9 × 7 m (16 × 23 ft)—that special trucks had to be requisitioned. Nothing about this process was easy; in the course of its evacuation the painting became ensnarled in the trolley line wires of the town of Versailles.

Louvre workers carefully pack some of the museum's masterpieces into shipping crates that were then evacuated to various repositories outside the city. The painting visible in the foreground is *The Young Beggar* by Bartolomé Esteban Murillo, one of Spain's greatest painters. In the photograph at left, Louvre workmen prepare the *Venus de Milo* for crating.

Opposite

The Grand Galerie at the Louvre after removal of its treasures.

On the Road
The Château at Chambord
was the first storage
destination for Louvre
masterpieces. It would not be
the last.
Late 1939

Many of the Louvre artworks were stored at the Château de Sourches, near Le Mans. Out of an abundance of caution, officials placed huge letters spelling out "Musée du Louvre" on the lawn, visible to pilots overhead. Signs were also posted on the gates identifying the Château as the residence of many of the Louvre's treasures. In the photograph below, workers prepare to dismount Charles Le Brun's portrait of *Pierre Séguier, Le Chancelier de France*, a massive canvas measuring 3.1 × 3.4 m (10 × 11 ft).

HOLLAND

Rijksmuseum Evacuation
Upon news of the signing of the German-Russian Non-Aggression Pact on August 23, 1939, officials at the Rijksmuseum in Amsterdam acted quickly. In the photograph above, Old Master paintings have been removed from the walls and stacked awaiting shipment. Prior to being loaded onto trucks for evacuation, they were inventoried by museum staff. Furniture vans were required for the transport of crated works of art as they were the largest vehicles available to quickly move size and bulk to safety.

The Wartime Odyssey of Rembrandt's *Nightwatch*

The three photographs at right depict the movement of the *Nightwatch* during the war. After being removed from its first shelter in Castricum, the *Nightwatch* was carried into a bombproof vault in Heemskerk under the watchful eye of uniformed German personnel in March, 1941.

Rembrandt's *Nightwatch* was moved on March 24, 1942, to the mountain shelter at St. Pietersberg near Maastricht along the Dutch-German border (center right).

The *Nightwatch* was kept rolled-up inside the St. Pietersberg shelter. Though perhaps shocking today, the rolling of this massive canvas 3.4 × 4.3 m (11 × 14 ft) was the most efficient means of safeguarding and transporting Rembrandt's masterpiece. The *Nightwatch* was finally taken to a specially constructed, bombproof shelter at Paaslo (lower right), where it was kept until June, 1945.

When Allied Forces liberated Holland, the *Nightwatch* was returned by special boat through the Dutch canal system where it was secretly delivered to the Rijksmuseum for a formal unrolling ceremony on June 30, 1945. In the center of the canvas, note the figure of Captain Frans Banning Cocq and his elegant lace collar, a symbol of social status in 17th-century Holland.

Homecoming

After being unrolled and reattached to its
stretcher for support, the painting is carefully
reviewed by officials, left to right: Professors
Reuling and Wolter of the Committee of
Amsterdam; Dr. C. Lindeman, a director of the
Rijksmuseum; D.C. Roell, general director of the
Rijksmuseum; and (second from right) the Dutch
painter Ruter, also a member of the Committee of
Amsterdam.

Rembrandt van Rijn, *Nightwatch*
(Militia Company of Captain Frans Banning Cocq),
1642.

Oil on canvas, 3.6 × 4.4 m (10 ft 10 in × 14 ft 4 in).
Rijksmuseum, Amsterdam.

ITALY

Florence

Because of its enormous height and weight, Michelangelo's epic *David* could not be removed from the Accademia. Once again, ingenuity won the day as local craftsmen wrapped the marble structure, then entombed it with sand and brick.

This is the scene that would have greeted a wartime visitor to the Accademia: *David* has been entombed along with the adjacent sculptures by Michelangelo. These works are collectively known as the *Captives*, or *Slaves*, because the artist left the figures unfinished in their marble blocks.

Piazza Signoria

To safeguard the numerous sculptural treasures in the Loggia dei Lanzi, Florentine officials removed the works from their pediments and stored some on site in bricked shelters, while shipping others to various repositories in the Tuscan hillside.

The photograph on the left shows the Loggia dei Lanzi as it appears today, with famous Renaissance sculptures by Cellini and Giambologna.

Ingenuity was constantly used to protect artworks, in particular those whose shape or position did not permit simple crating. Donatello's extraordinary pulpit in the Church of San Lorenzo was entombed in brick much the same way as was the *David*.

Rome

Another of Michelangelo's masterpieces, *Moses*, was wrapped in protective cloth and entombed by brick. The impressive marble sculpture, created by Michelangelo for the Tomb of Pope Julius II, is almost 2.4 m (8 ft) in height.

<small>OPPOSITE</small>

Michelangelo, *Moses*, 1513-16 and 1542-45.
Marble, H. 2.3 m (7 ft 8 in).
San Pietro in Vincoli, Rome.

Roman Monuments

No object was too large to protect. In the photographs on the left, the Arch of Constantine and Trajan's Column are protected. Note the Colosseum behind the Arch of Constantine. The photographs on the right show the monuments as they appear today.
1940-1941

Venice

The magnificent Piazza San Marco has always been the center of activity for visitors. In this photograph a wooden façade has been constructed to protect the front of the Church of St. Mark's. The great skill of Italian craftsmen almost made it appear as part of the permanent structure.

Protection By All Means

Italian officials made every effort to ensure the survival of each masterpiece. The photograph at left shows the *Assumption of the Virgin* by Giambattista Tiepolo, a ceiling fresco in the Chiesa della Purità in Udine. Note the many rows of pews beneath the protective scaffolding. The photograph below shows the careful rolling of Tintoretto's massive painting of the *Last Supper* in San Stefano, Venice. The canvas is 3.4 × 5.2 m (11 × 17 ft).

Evacuation by Barge

The waterways and canals of Venice have always presented unique transportation issues, none more so than the removal of artworks for safekeeping. These photographs show how workers used skids to position crated paintings onto trucks, which were then transported by a barge.

RUSSIA

Leningrad (St. Petersburg)
This statue of Peter the Great, known as the *Bronze Horseman*, was protected by wooden encasement. In the background is the great St. Isaac's Cathedral.
1941

Hermitage Evacuation

The vast holdings of the Hermitage Museum required both staff and volunteers to work around the clock in order to protect the collection.

The Rembrandt Room of the Hermitage includes at least 24 paintings by the Dutch master, including his tour-de-force, *Return of the Prodigal Son*, which was the only picture in the Hermitage Museum to receive its own crate. Paintings on canvas were hurriedly removed from their frames, then rolled like maps before being crated. The photograph above shows what awaits today's visitors to the Hermitage Museum.

The Tent Hall Room of the Hermitage Museum, as it looked after the removal of its extraordinary collection of Dutch Old Master paintings. In the foreground is a pile of sand with a shovel, used in the event of a fire. This was a common sight in each room. But for the paintings having been returned to their frames, this room looks virtually unchanged today.

THE UNITED STATES

National Gallery of Art

President Roosevelt dedicated the new National Gallery of Art, so generously conceived and paid for by Andrew W. Mellon, who then donated it along with his art collection to the nation. Subsequent significant donations were made by other great American art collectors, including Samuel Kress and Joseph E. Widener. The National Gallery is unique among its counterparts in the world for several reasons. Its governing structure consists of a small board which includes the Chief Justice of the United States and the Secretaries of Treasury and State. Its entire collection is comprised of donations and, to a much lesser extent, select purchases using privately donated funds. Not a single acquisition has been purchased with government money. There are no artworks in the collection that were acquired by military conquest.

"It is for this reason that the people of America accept the inheritance of these ancient arts. Whatever these paintings may have been to men who looked at them a generation back—today they are not only works of art. Today they are the symbols of the human spirit, and of the world the freedom of the human spirit made—a world against which armies now are raised and countries overrun and men imprisoned and their work destroyed.

To accept, today, the work of German painters such as Holbein and Dürer and of Italians like Botticelli and Raphael, and of painters of the low countries like Van Dyck and Rembrandt, and of famous Frenchmen, famous Spaniards—to accept this work today on behalf of the people of this democratic nation is to assert the belief of the people of this nation in a human spirit which now is everywhere endangered and which, in many countries where it first found form and meaning, has been rooted out and broken and destroyed.

To accept this work today is to assert the purpose of the people of America that the freedom of the human spirit and human mind which has produced the world's great art and all its science—shall not be utterly destroyed."

PRESIDENT FRANKLIN D. ROOSEVELT

REMARKS MADE AT THE DEDICATION CEREMONY OF THE NATIONAL GALLERY OF ART, WASHINGTON, D.C.

March 17, 1941

The Biltmore Estate

Constructed by George Washington Vanderbilt III from 1889-95, the Biltmore Estate is nestled among over 100,000 acres of forest just outside Asheville, North Carolina. Its remote location, with nearby rail access, made it an ideal storage facility for the 75 masterpieces evacuated from the National Gallery. As the trucks arrived with these treasures, they were greeted by custodians who supervised their off-loading and storage.

January 1942

WAR ARRIVES

"The destruction of Poland has priority...even if war breaks out in the West, the destruction of Poland remains the priority.... I shall give a propagandist reason for starting the war no matter whether it is plausible or not. The victor will not be asked afterwards whether he told the truth or not. When starting and waging war, it is not right that matters but victory. Close your hearts to pity. Act brutally."

ADOLF HITLER, REMARKS MADE TO SENIOR COMMANDERS OF THE ARMED SERVICES BERGHOF, BERCHTESGADEN

"...we shall seek no terms, we shall tolerate no parley; we may show mercy—we shall ask for none."

PRIME MINISTER SIR WINSTON CHURCHILL, BBC BROADCAST JULY 14, 1940

Adolf Hitler and his entourage visited the conquered "City of Light" in June of 1940 on the Führer's one and only trip to Paris. He squeezed into his three-hour visit the most popular tourist sites, including the Opéra, the Madeleine, Arc de Triomphe, Sacré-Coeur, and the Eiffel Tower. Accompanying Hitler are, from left: SS leader Karl Wolff, architects Hermann Giesler and Albert Speer; behind are General Wilhelm Keitel and SS Adjutant Wilhelm Brückner.

World War II officially began on September 1, 1939, with the German invasion of Poland. Blitzkrieg was a new form of attack that had devastating consequences in Poland, nowhere more so that in its capital city of Warsaw. Nazi Germany's surprise attack served as the final proclamation to the world of Hitler's intentions. To say that Hitler detested the Poles would be an understatement of epic proportion. The Poles, like the Russians and other Slavic peoples were, in Hitler's mind, inferior races that he was determined to destroy. Polish residents would be deported to an area known as the Government-General, which would be administered by Hitler protégé Hans Frank. Most would never return home. The Western half of the country would become expansion space for citizens of the Reich.

Fortunately, some preparations by Polish museums and collectors were already underway when German troops invaded on September 1. Certain private collections, such as that of the Czartoryski family, which included works by Leonardo da Vinci, Raphael, and Rembrandt, were hidden in country houses or sent to other museums for safekeeping. Churches and synagogues dismantled their altars and other important relics, then attempted to hide the most valuable items. It was, in the end, too little, too late. By September 17, Hitler, enraged over the resistance of Warsaw's citizens, personally directed incendiary bombing of the city's historic center. Damage to the Warsaw Royal Castle was significant. The city itself was devastated and, after renewed bombing in 1944, was for all practical purposes destroyed.

In contrast to the Slavic city of Warsaw, Hitler considered Cracow to be "Germanic." The consequences of this distinction were dramatic. Between 1939 to 1944, Warsaw's population decreased from 1,300,000 residents to only 164,000. Ninety percent of the historic and commercial buildings and health facilities and about seventy percent of the schools, universities, and residential buildings were in ruins. By contrast, Cracow, which had become the headquarters for Governor-General Hans Frank and his administration, incurred very little damage.

As was the case with Warsaw, resistance against the invading Germans exacted a disastrous toll on the city of Rotterdam. On May 14, 1940, after a week of fierce fighting, Dutch officials entered into surrender discussions with the Germans. Not satisfied with the pace of these discussions, General Kurt Student ordered Luftwaffe bombing of the historic center of Rotterdam. More than 800 people were killed; damage to the city was severe. Fortuitously, the Boymans Museum, which housed one of Holland's great collections, was not damaged.

Paris was spared the fate of Warsaw and Rotterdam due in part to the French government's decision to end the fighting against the vastly superior German army and enter into an armistice. Unlike Warsaw and other Eastern cities, Hitler and others in the Nazi regime secretly admired France for its culture and civilization, in particular the city of Paris. Still, conquering France had to precede enjoyment of it. Hitler's determination to first degrade and humiliate his opponents before subjugating them to his will was never more apparent than at the formal surrender ceremony in Compiègne on June 22, 1940. For four long years the Parisians would endure the hardships of being an occupied city.

Once war commenced, England was resolute in its opposition to Hitler. Encouraged by Göring, the Führer believed England could be bombed into submission. London was a key target. Once again, the bombing campaigns and subsequent fires caused horrific damage to the city's most famous monuments. Americans need only remember their feelings upon seeing a partially destroyed Pentagon in Washington, D.C., on September 11, 2001, to imagine how Londoners must have felt to see the Queen of England walking across the rubble of bomb-damaged Buckingham Palace in 1940.

While not a major engagement, Germany's conquest of Greece and occupation of Athens in April, 1941, after three weeks of fighting, was tinged with irony. The recurring use of the classic Greek figure in art of the Third Reich and the sight of the Nazi swastika being raised above the great Acropolis created a stark contrast between the philosophies of Hitler's despotism and ancient Greece's democratic idealism. Germany's entry into Greece was necessitated by the risk of Italian troops capitulating to Greek and British forces. This would not be the last time Hitler's confidence in Mussolini and the Italian Army was misplaced.

The German-Russian Non-Aggression Pact of August 1939 had, by 1941, served its purpose. During that period, Hitler annexed a large portion of Poland to the Reich without precipitating a war with the Soviets. He was then able to focus on his Western ambitions in France, Belgium, Holland, and, of course, England. Emboldened by this success, with no obstacle seeming too large to overcome, Hitler issued the following secret order to officers through the Chief of the Naval Staff:

The Führer has decided to erase from the face of the earth St. Petersburg. The existence of this large city will have no further interest after Soviet Russia is destroyed…. It is proposed to approach near to the city and to destroy it with the aid of an artillery barrage from weapons of different calibers and long air attacks…. The problem of the life of the population and the provisioning of them is a problem which cannot and must not be decided by us. In this war… we are not interested in preserving even a part of the population of this large city.

Russia was militarily unprepared for Operation Barbarossa—Germany's invasion of Russia on June 22, 1941. The now battle-hardened German Army reached the outskirts of Leningrad within days. The great palaces of Peterhof and Pavlovsk were looted, then severely damaged. Gilded fountains of Peterhof were dismantled and transported back to Germany along with 5,000 pieces of antique furniture and 35,000 works of art. Thus began the German Army's 900-day siege of Leningrad during which time all supplies to the city were cut off; the city was shelled relentlessly. Through three excruciatingly cold winters the citizens endured unimaginable hardships and suffering. As many as one million civilians died from starvation and bombardment. Throughout this ordeal, however, the treasures of the Hermitage were protected in a demonstration of the courage and sacrifice that would characterize the Russian struggle to survive Hitler's scorched-earth policy.

WARSAW

Hitler ordered the bombing of the Royal Castle which resulted in the fire seen above. Kazimierz Brokle, curator of the Castle, was killed in the courtyard. In the weeks that followed, volunteers salvaged surviving artworks and placed them in the National Museum. The historic tower was partially destroyed and the roof completely burned. This was the first phase of the Castle's destruction. (For the complete sequence of destruction, see page 272.)
September 1939

Using Jewish prisoners, German soldiers directed the drilling of holes in which dynamite sticks were placed to complete the ultimate destruction of the Castle in 1944.

Inside the Royal Castle
Courageous castle officials attempt to put out a fire in
the ballroom. In the aftermath of Nazi destruction,
thousands of priceless books and archives are strewn
across the vast floor of the library.
September 1939

CRACOW

Wawel Castle under German Occupation

Governor-General Hans Frank, Hitler's protégé and
commander of German forces in Poland, enjoyed every
luxury possible. He established his headquarters at the
Wawel Castle and used its courtyard for military
parades and celebrations.

It was no small irony that the former
"Press Palace" was converted by the
Nazis into the headquarters for "Popular
Education and Propaganda," bedecked in
the same Nazi banners that quickly
spread throughout the conquered city.

Erasing Polish Culture

As part of Nazi policy, the history of Poland's artists, writers, and composers was to be erased. These photographs show the monument to Poland's greatest poet, Adam Mickiewiez, being pushed from its lofty pediment by a group of German laborers that had been sent from the Reich expressly for the destruction of Polish monuments.

A bronze monument to Poland's greatest musician, Frederic Chopin, was designed by Waclaw Syzmanowski and erected in Warsaw in 1910. It was destroyed by the Nazis in May 1941, at the command of Governor-General Frank. The photograph below shows the monument after it was dissected and placed on a flatbed railcar for transport to a smelter.

ROTTERDAM

Frustrated with the pace of surrender discussions, German military officials ordered the Luftwaffe to bomb the historic city center. This photograph shows the Boymans Museum (now the Boymans-Van Beuningen Museum) in front of the billowing smoke of fires caused by the bombing. Because the museum was located far enough away from the city center, it avoided damage. Within the historic center, only the Church of Saint Lawrence, or Sint-Laurenskerk, was left standing.
May 1940

PARIS

Der FÜHRER am Grabe Napoleons

History Repeating
Hitler's whirlwind visit to Paris included a number of stops by his motorcade, none more significant then his visit to Les Invalides, resting place of Napoleon's tomb. Upon gazing at the tomb of his hero, Hitler was heard to remark, "This is the finest moment of my life."
June 1940

German Occupation

German troops proudly hung the Nazi flag from the Arc de Triomphe.

LONDON

The Blitz
Prime Minister Sir Winston Churchill assesses damage to the House of Commons.
May 1940

Queen Elizabeth and King George IV inspect damage to Buckingham Palace caused by German bombing.
September 1940

Approximately 40,000 British civilians were killed by German bombing. Had it not been for the tunnels of the subway system, which proved to be effective air-raid shelters, the death toll would have been higher.
October 1940

ATHENS

Atop the Acropolis, with the Parthenon as the backdrop, German infantrymen prepare to raise the Nazi Swastika after their successful and brief invasion of Greece. At the far right a German soldier fires his pistol into the air.
April 1941

After Germany's occupation of Greece, these three
Dornier Bombers (DO-17s) participated in an air
parade over the Acropolis.
May 1941

LENINGRAD (ST. PETERSBURG)

Workers attempt to repair a hole in the floor of the Hermitage caused by German bombing. In the photograph below, historic coaches stored in the coachyard at the Hermitage were destroyed by a 70mm shell blast.

Siege of Leningrad: Siege of Art
German bombs and artillery aimed at Leningrad also targeted the Hermitage Museum causing considerable damage to the museum. Note the hole in the ceiling of the Rastrelli Gallery.

OPPOSITE

Russian officials prepare to defend Leningrad against the German invaders. In the background is the towering dome of St. Isaac's Cathedral.
Summer 1942

THEFT BY ANY OTHER NAME

CHAPTER 4

"We now have to face the task of cutting up the cake according to our needs in order to be able: first, to dominate it; second, to administer it; third, to exploit it."

ADOLF HITLER, MEETING WITH GERMAN LEADERS INCLUDING HERMANN GÖRING, ALFRED ROSENBERG AND MARTIN BORMANN, JULY 16, 1941

"My pictures, in the collections which I have bought in the course of years, have never been collected for private purposes, but only for the extension of a gallery in my home town of Linz a.d. Donau."

ADOLF HITLER, APRIL 29, 1945, PRIVATE WILL AND TESTAMENT WRITTEN TWO HOURS BEFORE HE COMMITTED SUICIDE.

"It [exploitation] used to be called plundering. But today things have become more humane. In spite of that, I intend to plunder, and to do it thoroughly."

HERMANN GÖRING, SPEAKING TO A CONFERENCE OF NAZI OCCUPATION COMMISSIONERS, AUGUST 6, 1942

Members of the Hermann Göring Tank Division evacuate paintings from Monte Cassino. Italian officials later discovered that fifteen cases of art had been stolen.
October 1943

Hitler and the Nazis were not the first to plunder the spoils of those they conquered. Neither were they the first to develop shopping lists of cultural objects and treasures prior to the outbreak of war. They were, however, the first to so thoroughly and systematically organize the theft of others' possessions. For more than seven years, they stole at will. When laws blocked their ambitions, they changed them. When people resisted, they threatened, or worse, killed them, then took the objects of their desire by force. While undeniably despicable, their accomplishment was extraordinary. Looting during the Third Reich became institutionalized; it was official policy.

The looting of Europe by Hitler, Göring, and the Nazis was initially focused on works of art designated for Hitler's Linz Museum or other regional Austrian and German museums. Göring also targeted artworks destined for his country estate known as Carinhall. The scope was quickly expanded to achieve political and cultural objectives such as the denigration of Jews, Poles, and other Slavs. By 1940, the Nazis were stealing virtually anything of value from their victims in Eastern Europe while accumulating the confiscated belongings (mostly of Jews) in Western Europe for future shipment and use as needed. Words such as "safeguarded," "secured," "purchased," "traded," and "confiscated" were frequently used as euphemisms for induced, bribed, coerced, and stolen. In the seven year period from 1938-1945, Hitler and the Nazis stole millions of items including some of the greatest art treasures of Western civilization.

With the annexation of Austria on March 12, 1938, Hitler wasted no time in fulfilling his dreams for the Linz Museum. Within days he had confiscated the collections of Vienna's most prominent Jewish families such as Rothschild and Bloch-Bauer. Some families managed to flee Austria in advance of the German troops, thus leaving their belongings "ownerless" in the eyes of Nazi officials. Thereafter, theft and looting was not random; it was far worse. German law now governed day–to-day life in Austria. As such, the Nazis had merely to implement their opportunistic laws to "legally" obtain that which they desired. The floodgate was now propped open.

Poland was far less "fortunate" than Austria. According to Hitler's orders, the Polish people and its culture were to be exterminated and replaced with a "New Order," i.e., one based on Hitler's racial theories. Important non-Polish artworks were located and spirited out of the country as fast as the German troops occupied it. The altarpiece of Veit Stoss in Cracow, considered one of the world's greatest works of art, was shipped to Nuremberg within five weeks of the invasion. At the top of Hitler's shopping list was the priceless Czartoryski Collection, found hidden in a wall of the family's country house in Sienawa, then stolen. The arrival of SS Lieutenant Col. Dr. Kajetan Mühlmann, who was also the Special Delegate for the Securing of Art and Cultural Goods, sealed Poland's fate.

The most extensive art looting organization within the Third Reich was undoubtedly the ERR (Einsatzstab Reichsleiter Rosenberg) led by Alfred Rosenberg. Originally created to gather political material in occupied territories for propagandist use against enemies of the Reich, its mandate shifted to the seizure of Jewish owned art collections in France. As part of their anti-Semitic policy, the Nazis decreed in September, 1940, that Jews no longer had the rights of citizenship. It followed then that they had no property rights. Their belongings, from the simplest of possessions—beds, furniture, children's toys—to priceless collections of art, became "ownerless." Accordingly, the Nazis considered that their subsequent gathering and collection of these Jewish owned assets was lawful. All confiscated artworks were to be inventoried and made available for Nazi collectors or filtered into the art trade.

Although the authority of the ERR emanated from Hitler, operations were frequently usurped by Göring whose collecting ambitions had no bounds. This was a delicate balancing act for the Reichmarshall as he knew that the very best artworks must first be offered to the Führer. However, the wealth of art in France and, in particular, that owned by Jewish collectors—who were also the most outstanding art dealers of their time—was too tempting to ignore. Thousands of objects, even entire collections, were seized from French Jewish owners by the ERR, many of which were then deposited at the Jeu de Paume museum.

The Jeu de Paume, a small building near the Louvre in the Tuileries Gardens, soon became a veritable warehouse of priceless treasures during the war. It was staffed by ERR personnel and, most importantly, Louvre curator Rose Valland, the heroine of the French museums, who secretly kept track of all the looted objects that passed through its doors. From his first visit to the Jeu de Paume on November 3, 1940, to his last on November 27, 1942, Göring made twenty separate visits on twelve trips to Paris. He was usually accompanied by Walter Andreas Hofer, his chief art buyer and personal curator. In all, Göring and his agents would "remove" over 700 works of art from the Jeu de Paume for his personal collection.

Italy presented a somewhat unique situation in as much as it began the war as an ally of Germany. As early as 1937, Hitler had advisors in Italy to identify works of art that should be acquired. One piece in particular, a Roman statue known as the Lancellotti *Discobolus* (or discus-thrower), had caught the Führer's eye. Hitler had to overcome the considerable opposition of certain Italian officials to persuade Mussolini and Italian Foreign Minister, Count Galeazzo Ciano, to allow the private sale and export to Munich of the *Discobolus*, long recognized by the Italians as a masterpiece of Italian culture and thus barred from export. Other such artworks would follow a similar path out of Italy until July, 1943, when the Allied invasion of Europe commenced in Sicily. Just two months later, Italy surrendered and joined forces with the Allies. With Mussolini gone, Hitler had to utilize other methods to add to his collection.

For a period of time thereafter, German officials made a concerted effort to characterize their removal and relocation of art as a "safeguarding" operation. In October, 1943, German troops removed paintings, books and other important items from the monastery at Monte Cassino, located atop a mountain about one and a half hours southeast of Rome. After strenuous protests by Italian officials, they delivered these treasures to officials at the Vatican in January, 1944, in a well-publicized and choreographed event. German propaganda films went to great lengths to portray this as an example of German army efforts to protect treasures from the "barbarian" American army. What wasn't disclosed at the time was the prior removal of fifteen crates of paintings by officers of the Hermann Göring Tank Division. These works from the Capodimonte Museum in Naples, including masterpieces by Titian, Pieter Brueghel, Claude Lorrain, Palma Vecchio, and Raphael, had been delivered to Göring in December, 1943, as a birthday gift. Much as he would have liked to add them to his immense collection, Göring understood that the amount of attention focused on these paintings precluded his acceptance. He thus had them stored in a repository in Austria which also contained innumerable artworks intended for the Führer museum and other regional museums.

The increasingly desperate military situation in Italy resulted in more overt acts of theft of key art treasures by German officials. The pretense of "safeguarding" works became more transparent than ever. Artworks from the Uffizi, Bargello, and Palazzo Pitti in Florence, including iconic works by Donatello, Botticelli, Michelangelo, and Titian, were hurriedly removed from repositories in nearby country villas and loaded onto open-top trucks with virtually no packing materials. As the German army retreated north towards home, they took with them more than 500 of these stolen paintings. Ultimately, their use as a bargaining chip by SS General Wolff in secret discussions concerning the surrender of German forces in Italy delayed and, as events unfolded, prevented their crossing the Italian border into German controlled Austria. The artworks were only twenty-five miles from the Austrian border when they were located by Monuments officers, soldiers from United States Fifth Army, and Italian Fine Arts specialists.

Nazi destruction of Russian monuments was quite deliberate, just as it had been in Poland. While many cultural treasures were stolen, many more were obliterated as part of Hitler's scorched-earth policy in the Soviet Union. During the three years of German occupation, no less than 427 museums, 1,670 Russian Orthodox churches, 237 Catholic churches, and 532 synagogues were looted or destroyed. The complete disregard for art treasures contained in many of these destroyed structures illustrated Hitler's utter contempt for the Russian people and their varied cultures. One notable exception were the wall panels from the Amber Room, stolen by German troops from Catherine Palace at Tsarskoye Selo, located about twelve miles outside Leningrad. Having been a gift from the King of Prussia to Peter the Great in 1716, the Amber panels were a coveted prize both for their unique beauty and German origin.

"They...tried to paint a picture of me as a looter of art treasures. In the first place, during a war everybody loots a little bit...."

HERMANN GÖRING, INTERVIEW GIVEN TO U.S. ARMY PSYCHIATRIST DR. LEON GOLDENSOHN AT THE NUREMBERG JAILS DURING THE FIRST OF THE WAR CRIME TRIALS, MAY 28, 1946

Cracow

Governor-General Frank visited the pre-historic section of the Institute for German
East Work (*Institut für Deutsche Ostarbeit*). The organization's excavation work in
Poland was designed to "prove" Poles were intruders in areas that were once ancient
German settlements.

The *Ahnenerbe*

Gestapo Chief Heinrich Himmler (center), oversaw the work of the *Ahnenerbe*, an archeological unit of the SS created in 1935. Its purpose was to provide evidence of German superiority by proving that all other cultures had German origins. Their efforts backfired: the results undermined their very objective, something even Hitler acknowledged in great frustration.

POLAND

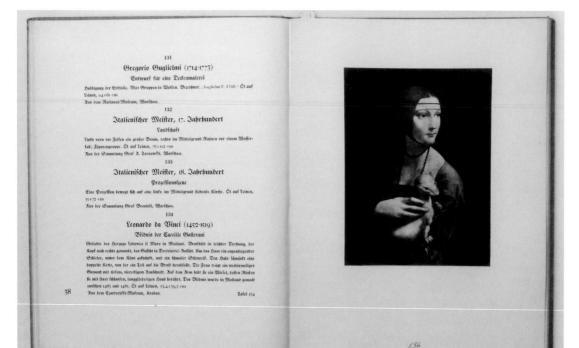

Premeditated Theft

Nazi officials in Poland, particularly Kajetan Mühlmann, prepared special detailed catalogues of artworks to be "obtained." In the photograph above, an elaborate box contained loose reproductions of desired artworks. The photographs on the left show the catalogue of Polish art treasures open to the two most famous paintings in Poland: Leonardo da Vinci's *Lady With an Ermine* and Raphael's *Portrait of a Young Man*, both from the Czartoryski Collection in Cracow. These priceless masterpieces were at the top of the Nazi "shopping list." Mühlmann personally delivered both to Göring, but after an argument erupted between Göring and Governor-General Frank over who was going to keep the paintings, Mühlmann was ordered to return them to him for temporary custody in Cracow. When the Allies captured Frank, only the painting by Leonardo was in his possession.

Wawel Castle, Cracow

Veit Stoss

The great Veit Stoss altarpiece in the Church of Our Lady. Polish officials hurriedly disassembled and spirited it away for safekeeping from the advancing German forces. Nazi officials quickly located it. On December 16 it was transported to Nuremberg, birthplace of Veit Stoss. The photograph to the right provides the same perspective, however in place of the Veit Stoss masterwork is a quite inferior altarpiece placed there by German officials.
Cracow 1939

In an undated report by Dr. Hans Posse, director of the Dresden Gemäldegalerie, he wrote the following: "I was able to gain some knowledge on the public and private collections, as well as clerical property, in Cracow and Warsaw. It is true that we cannot hope too much to enrich ourselves from the acquisition of great art works of paintings and sculptures, with exception of the Veit Stoss altar and the plates of Hans von Kulmbach in the Church of Maria in Cracow… and several other works from the National Museum in Warsaw."

During the brutal Nazi occupation of Poland, all artworks were stripped from the National Museum in Cracow. The photograph on the left shows the museum as it appeared before the war, while the photograph below shows the same space being used by the Nazis for propaganda exhibitions.

HOLLAND

Amsterdam
Göring considered himself a connoisseur and made a point of visiting shops and galleries when he traveled outside Germany. Even while the Nazi war machine marched across Europe, Göring is seen here shopping for jewelry.
Summer 1940

FRANCE

"On Wednesday, 5 February 1941, I was ordered to the Jeu de Paume by the Reich Marshal. At 1500 o'clock, the Reich Marshal, accompanied by General Hanesse, Herr Angerer, and Herr Hofer, visited the exhibition of Jewish art treasures newly set up there.... Then with me as his guide, the Reich Marshal inspected the exhibited art treasures and made a selection of those works of art which were to go to the Führer, and those which were to be placed in his own collection. During this confidential conversation, I again called the Reich Marshal's attention to the fact that a note of protest had been received from the French Government against the activity of the Einsatzstab Rosenberg, with reference to the Hague Rules on Land Warfare recognized by Germany at the Armistice of Compiègne and I pointed out that General Von Stülpnagel's interpretation of the manner in which the confiscated Jewish art treasures are to be treated, was apparently contrary to the Reich Marshal's interpretation. Thereupon, the Reich Marshal asked for a detailed explanation and gave the following orders: 'First, it is my orders that you have to follow. You will act directly according to my orders. The art collected in the Jeu de Paume is to be loaded on a special train immediately and taken to Germany by order of the Reich Marshal...

CONTINUED AT TOP OF PAGE 115

Jeu de Paume, Paris
The Jeu de Paume, once a revered center for contemporary art in the 1920s and 1930s, became the central depot for art stolen by the ERR (Einsatzstab Reichsleiter Rosenberg).

…These art objects which are to go in the Führer's possession, and those art objects which the Reich Marshal claims for himself, will be loaded on two railroad cars which will be attached to the Reich Marshal special trains, and upon his departure for Germany, at the beginning of next week, will be taken along to Berlin. Feldführer Von Behr will accompany the Reich Marshal in his special train on the journey to Berlin.' When I made the objection that the jurists would probably be of different opinion and that protests would most likely be made by the military commander in France, the Reich Marshal answered, saying verbatim as follows, 'Dear Bunjes let me worry about that; I am the highest jurist in the State.' The Reich Marshal promised to send from his headquarters by courier to the Chief of the Military Administrative District of Paris on Thursday, 6 February, the written order for the transfer to Germany of the confiscated Jewish art treasures."

A LETTER FROM DR. BUNJES PRODUCED AS EVIDENCE AT THE NUREMBERG TRIALS

Göring made twenty visits to the Jeu de Paume between November 1940 and November 1942. On some occasions he visited in civilian clothes, others in one of his various uniforms. The scene inside remained much the same: admiration and selection of desired works to add to his collection and the Führer's, while enjoying the best Paris had to offer, in this instance a glass of champagne and a cigar.

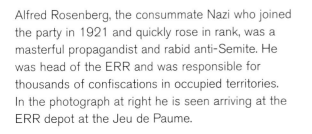

Alfred Rosenberg, the consummate Nazi who joined the party in 1921 and quickly rose in rank, was a masterful propagandist and rabid anti-Semite. He was head of the ERR and was responsible for thousands of confiscations in occupied territories. In the photograph at right he is seen arriving at the ERR depot at the Jeu de Paume.

"M-Aktion"

These photographs document the extent of Nazi looting as carried out by the ERR. "M-Aktion" was a plan designed by the ERR to steal massive quantities of household goods and furniture for use in the eastern occupied territories. This resulted in the confiscation of hundreds of thousands of personal and household items including furniture, pianos, and even children's toys.

"The confiscation of Jewish homes was carried out as follows: When no records were available of the addresses of Jews who had fled or departed, as was the case, for instance, in Paris, so-called requisitioning officials went from house to house in order to collect information as to abandoned Jewish homes. They drew up inventories of these homes and sealed them. In Paris alone, about twenty requisitioning officials requisitioned more than 38,000 homes. The transportation of these homes were completed with all the available vehicles of the Union of Parisian Moving Contractors who had to provide up to 150 trucks, and 1,200 to 1,500 laborers daily."

REPORT SUBMITTED BY THE DIRECTOR OF ROSENBERG'S OFFICE WEST AT THE NUREMBERG TRIALS

Stolen Loot

"M-Aktion" loot in a Parisian depot awaits shipment east. "52,828 Jewish lodgings were seized and sealed in favor of the bombed-out victims [i.e., homeless Germans]. Including special orders, furniture has been removed from 47,569 dwellings for shipment to the bombed cities... 69,619 Jewish lodgings were looted, that the furniture occupied over 1 million cubic meters, and that it took 26,984 freight cars, that is 674 trains, to remove it."

ROSENBERG REPORT, DATED NOVEMBER 4, 1943, PRESENTED AS EVIDENCE AT THE NUREMBERG TRIALS

"It is quite true that I received a governmental order to confiscate archives, works of art, and later, household goods from Jewish citizens in France... I was informed that the Jewish people in question no longer inhabited their institutions, castles, and apartments...."

ALFRED ROSENBERG, TESTIMONY GIVEN AT THE NUREMBERG TRIALS

ITALY

On the day of this lavish reception held in Hitler's honor at the Palazzo Pitti in Florence by Italian leader Benito Mussolini, the Führer first learned of Italy's invasion of Greece.
October 1940

Partners in Crime
The nefarious relationship between the Führer and Mussolini made possible one of Hitler's greatest thefts of Italian art: the *Discobolus* (Discus-thrower).

The Führer poses in Munich with his newest art "acquisition"—the priceless *Discobolus*, removed from a Roman museum, then exported to Germany in violation of Italian patrimony laws. This was another example of theft by any other name. After the war, the Allies returned the sculpture to Rome.
1938

In 1943, museum officials in Naples moved their most important artworks to the Abbey of Monte Cassino. In October of that year, the Hermann Göring Tank Division removed 187 cases of art to their headquarters in Spoleto, ostensibly "to protect the treasures from the Anglo-American barbarians." After three months of outcry by Italian officials, the Division transported the cases for "safekeeping" to the Vatican amid great pomp and circumstance. It would take months for Italian officials to realize the deception: select paintings—Naple's very best—had already been removed and then taken to Germany as a gift for Göring. Most of these paintings were later found at a repository in Austria. In the photograph above, young seminarians help unload paintings.

January 1944

Sleight of Hand

A German officer receives a certificate of gratitude
from the delegate of the (Italian) Ministry of National
Education, Alfonso Bartoli, for "rescuing" the art.
January 1944

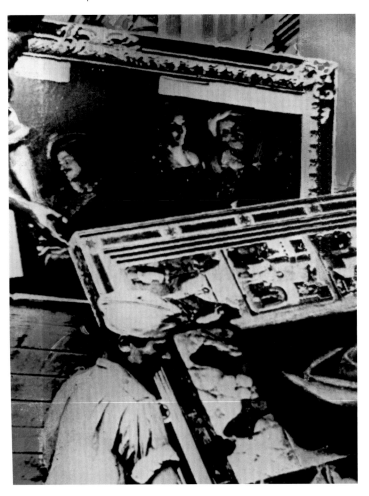

Overt Theft
Priceless art treasures from Florentine museums, which had been stored in neighboring Tuscan villas, were stolen by German troops as they retreated north towards Austria.

German soldiers steal Florentine art from a museum repository at the Oratory of Sant'Onofrio in Dicomano, 1944. The color photograph shows the Oratory as it appears today.

Florentine art treasures were hurriedly unloaded by retreating German troops and stored at the jail in San Leonardo, one of the last towns in northern Italy before crossing into German-controlled Austria.

In the photograph at right, Germans display Botticelli's masterpiece, *Camilla and the Centaur*, from the Uffizi.
1944

RUSSIA

"At Zarskoje Selo the company [of German commandos] seized and secured the property belonging to the palace-museum of the Empress Catherine. The Chinese silk draperies and the carved gilt ornaments were torn from the walls. The floor of artistic ornaments was dismantled and taken away. From the palace of the Emperor Alexander antique furniture and a large library containing some 6,000 to 7,000 volumes in French and over 5,000 volumes and manuscripts in Russian, were removed.... 'After the occupation of any big city, the leaders of these kommandos arrive, accompanied by various art experts. They inspect museums, picture galleries, exhibitions, and institutions of art and culture, they determine their condition and confiscate everything of value.'"

TESTIMONY GIVEN AT THE NUREMBERG TRIALS

Peterhof, known for its extraordinary system of guilded fountains that flow toward the Gulf of Finland, was stripped of its furniture, art objects, and fountains. All that remained was a hollow structure.

"The Army is interested in extinguishing fires only in such buildings as may be used for Army billets... All the rest to be destroyed; no historical or artistic buildings in the East to be of any value whatsoever."

ORDER ISSUED BY FIELD MARSHALL WALTER VON REICHENAU, AND APPROVED BY HITLER. DOCUMENT PRESENTED AT THE NUREMBERG TRIALS

These photographs of Catherine Palace show the scene of devastation after German troops had carted off the famed Amber Panels and gutted the structure. SEE PAGES 288-289.

HEROES AND HEROINES

CHAPTER 5

"Prior to this war, no army had thought of protecting the monuments of the country in which and with which it was at war, and there were no precedents to follow.... All this was changed by a general order issued by the Supreme Commander-in-chief [General Eisenhower] just before he left Algiers, an order accompanied by a personal letter to all Commanders...the good name of the Army depended in great measure on the respect which it showed to the art heritage of the modern world."

Lt. Col. Sir Leonard Woolley, Monuments, Fine Arts, and Archives Officer

"Shortly we will be fighting our way across the continent of Europe.... Inevitably, in the path of our advance will be found historical monuments and cultural centers which symbolize to the world all that we are fighting to preserve. It is the responsibility of every commander to protect and respect these symbols whenever possible."

Gen. Dwight D. Eisenhower, Letter to Field Commanders Prior to the Normandy Invasion, May 26, 1944

MFAA officer Capt. Walker Hancock assists residents of the town of La Gleize in Belgium with the relocation of the statue, known as *Madonna of La Gleize*, to a more secure site.

The endless list of villains stands in contrast to the number of heroes and heroines who protected, found, and restituted the greatest art treasures of Western civilization. Those who participated in the successful invasion of Europe and subsequent defeat of Nazi Germany and its allies deserve general recognition. European museum officials and many local volunteers certainly merit acknowledgment of and praise for their tireless efforts to minimize and, in some cases, avoid altogether damage to their collections and cultural monuments. Still, these monuments and artworks were the cultural patrimony of Europe. Far more surprising were the brave actions of a few others, mostly led by Americans and a key group of British officers, who at great personal sacrifice made every effort to protect the cultural treasures of others. But for their actions, Europe as we know it today might not exist.

127

Collectively, their role in perpetuating man's greatest creative gifts to future generations cannot be overstated.

As early as 1940, a small group of museum directors, curators, and scholars organized themselves as the "American Defense—Harvard Group." It was chaired by Dr. Paul Sachs, Associate Director of the Fogg Museum at Harvard. The Harvard Group was comprised of persons knowledgeable about art and cultural monuments, most of whom maintained contact with their European counterparts. These lines of communication would become invaluable sources of information as plans for the Allied invasion of Europe developed. All were concerned about the fate of Europe's cultural monuments and art treasures, a concern that was heightened by the fall of Paris to the Germans in June, 1940. The Harvard Group also included George Stout, Chief Conservator at the Fogg Museum and widely considered one of the nation's foremost experts on the protection of works of art. In time, Stout would become a significant figure in the planning and implementation of procedures used by officers in the field to protect, transport, and restitute the enormous mass of stolen artworks they would discover.

Other museum directors and officials were equally concerned about the protection of Europe's cultural treasures. Francis Henry Taylor, Director of the Metropolitan Museum in New York, already in contact with Sachs and Stout concerning these matters, traveled to Washington to meet with officials at the National Gallery. Governance of the National Gallery is somewhat unique. The by-laws stipulate that its board shall include the Chief Justice of the United States, the Secretary of State, and the Secretary of the Treasury. As such, it afforded Taylor and his colleagues near-direct access to White House officials, namely President Roosevelt. Their recommendation to Chief Justice Harlan F. Stone was to create "a corps of specialists to deal with the matter of protecting monuments and works of art in liaison with the Army and Navy." Chief Justice Stone agreed to chair a committee to study the protection of Europe's cultural treasures and to present the idea to FDR which he did in December, 1942.

In 1943 FDR and Prime Minister Churchill met in Casablanca where they reached the momentous decision to enter Europe via Italy, not France. As Allied Forces engaged opposing forces in Sicily and then the Italian mainland, military planners both in the field and in Washington were slow to realize the extraordinary damage that had and would continue to be done to cultural monuments in a combat zone. Given Italy's unique and abundant artistic riches it was difficult to know which structures had the greatest historic significance. The Nazi propaganda machine capitalized on this public relations ignorance and quickly produced newsreels and publications which portrayed the Americans as destroyers of European culture. Exacerbating this problem was damage caused by American and other Allied troops who frequently sought the lodging comforts of famous palaces and other important buildings. Allied military planners soon saw the importance of winning these propaganda battles and began to seek lists of cultural monuments and art treasures in occupied areas along with explanations of why they were important. The Harvard Group was contacted by Army officials and asked to generate such lists and to supply the names of men and women with expertise in these matters. Meanwhile, Taylor and others were urging the Civil Affairs Division of the Army to include experts on the preservation of historical monuments and art treasures in their detachments to each military theater.

In early 1943 yet another group, known as the American Council of Learned Societies, appointed a committee to address protection of Europe's art by identifying civilian experts who could liaise with the military. They also prepared pamphlets that detailed known German looting. All these groups' entreaties to government officials coalesced at about the same time. On June 23, 1943, FDR approved the formation of the "American Commission for the Protection and Salvage of Artistic and Historic Monuments in War Areas" widely known as "The Roberts Commission," after its chairman, Supreme Court Justice Owen J. Roberts. Thus was born the Monuments, Fine Arts, and Archives program ("MFAA") under the auspices of the Civil Affairs and Military Government Sections of the Allied Armies.

The "Venus Fixers" as they were sometimes called by fellow troops—"Monuments Men" by most others—were mostly young museum directors and curators, art professors and architects who volunteered for service. After the war, many would become leaders of the most prominent museums in the United States. Virtually every major American museum had one or more employee who served as an MFAA officer during World War II. Still, their numbers were ridiculously few when compared to the overwhelming task they confronted. In as much as the MFAA program was an untested concept, the Monuments Men had pathetically few resources to accomplish their job and little direction other than to inspect, repair, and report on monuments needing protection, and to prevent improper billeting by Allied troops in historic or culturally important buildings. This last task was a constant challenge. There was no handbook to follow. Those with skill or knowledge were given authority to act.

In addition to developing lists of monuments and other art treasures for use in war zones, MFAA officers prepared special aerial maps which identified critically important landmarks for American pilots to avoid on bombing missions. As Allied Forces secured towns in Sicily and those on the mainland, Monuments Men hustled any available vehicle to get to the most forward areas to assess damage. They also liaised with local officials to aid with repairs to prevent further damage from weather and vandals. Given the magnitude of damage coupled with severe personnel and supply shortages, the return of artworks from various hidden repositories to museums was an arduous process. As fighting moved north, Monuments Men discovered that priceless art treasures had been removed from museum repositories and churches by German soldiers. Thus began their investigation to locate and recover the stolen objects.

By the time of the D-Day Invasion of France on June 6, 1944, there were only twelve MFAA officers attached to American forces in Normandy. Damage in the area was severe, largely a result of Allied pre-invasion bombing and shelling. Their ability to assist with repairs was limited. Work consisted of preparing damage assessment reports and salvaging what remained. Similar situations awaited MFAA officers as Allied Forces fought their way into the heartlands of France, Belgium, and Luxembourg. By the time Allied Forces reached Germany, the totality of destruction caused their mission to shift from the protection of monuments to the search for moveable works of art. This would be their greatest achievement of the next five years as more than a thousand German repositories, many containing stolen art, would be found in Germany, Italy and Austria.

Select Leaders of Post-War American Institutions–All Former Monuments Men

Allen Memorial Art Museum, Oberlin, OH
Charles P. Parkhurst–Assistant Director, Chief Curator, and Director

American Association of Museums, Washington, D.C.
David E. Finley–President
Charles P. Parkhurst–President

Baltimore Museum of Art, MD
Charles P. Parkhurst–Director

Brooklyn Museum, NY
Frederick R. Pleasants–Curator
George N. Kates–Curator
Sheldon W. Keck–Conservator

Cleveland Museum of Art, OH
Sherman E. Lee–Director
Dorothy G. Shepherd–Curator

College of William and Mary, Williamsburg, VA
Everett Parker Lesley, Jr.–Professor

Columbia University, NY
Ernest T. DeWald–Professor

Cooper Union Museum, NY
Calvin S. Hathaway–Director
Everett Parker Lesley, Jr.–Curator

The Frick Collection, NY
Harry D. Grier–Director

Harvard University, Cambridge, MA
Craig H. Smyth–Professor
Mason Hammond–Professor
Norman T. Newton–Professor

Harvard University, Fogg Art Museum, Cambridge, MA
Charles L. Kuhn–Curator
Charles F. Gallagher–Curator
George L. Stout–Chief Conservator
Langdon Warner–Curator

Harvard University, Villa I Tatti, Center for Italian Renaissance Studies, Florence
Craig H. Smyth–Director

Institute of Contemporary Art, Boston, MA
James Sachs Plaut–Director

Legion of Honor Museum, San Francisco, CA
Thomas C. Howe–Director

Library of Congress, Washington, D.C.
Edgar Breitenbach–Chief, Department of Prints and Photographs

Metropolitan Museum of Art, NY
James J. Rorimer–Director
Theodore Rousseau, Jr.–Curator
Edith A. Standen–Curator
Theodore A. Heinrich–Associate Curator

Minneapolis Institute of Arts, MN
Harry D. Grier–Director
Richard S. Davis–Director
Charles F. Gallagher–Senior Curator

Museum of Modern Art , NY
Andrew C. Ritchie–Director, Department of Painting and Sculpture

National Archives, Washington, D.C.
Seymour J. Pomrenze

National Gallery of Art, Washington, D.C.
Charles P. Parkhurst–Assistant Director and Chief Curator
Perry B. Cott–Chief Curator
Everett Parker Lesley, Jr.–Curator

National Gallery of Art, Center for Advanced Study in the Visual Arts, Washington, D.C.
Craig H. Smyth–Professor

Nelson-Atkins Museum of Art, Kansas City, MO
Paul Gardner–Director
Lawrence W.R. Sickman–Director

New York City Ballet, NY
Lincoln E. Kirstein–Founder and President

New York University, Institute of Fine Arts, NY
Craig H. Smyth–Professor

Old Dominion University, Norfolk, VA
Everett Parker Lesley, Jr.–Professor

Princeton University, Princeton, NJ
Ernest E. DeWald–Professor
Robert A. Koch–Professor
Charles P. Parkhurst–Assistant Director, Princeton Art Museum

Seattle Art Museum, WA
Sherman E. Lee–Assistant Director

State University of New York, Binghamton, NY
Kenneth C. Lindsay–Professor

Toledo Museum of Art, OH
Otto Wittman–Director

University of California, Berkeley, CA
Walter W. Horn–Chairman, Department of Art
Bernard Taper–Professor of Journalism

University of Michigan Museum of Art, Ann Arbor, MI
Charles H. Sawyer–Director

University of Pennsylvania, Philadelphia, PA
Frederick Hartt–Professor

University of Virginia, Charlottesville, VA
Frederick Hartt–Professor

Washington University, St. Louis, MO
Frederick Hartt–Professor

Williams College Museum of Art, Williamstown, MA
S. Lane Faison–Director
Charles P. Parkhurst–Director

Worchester Art Museum, MA
George L. Stout–Conservator

Yale University Art Gallery, New Haven, CT
Theodore Sizer–Director
John M. Phillips–Director
Lamont Moore–Assistant Director
Andrew C. Ritchie–Director

Yale University, School of Art, New Haven, CT
Deane Keller–Professor
Charles H. Sawyer–Professor

TO ALLIED FORCES
NATIONAL MONUMENT

OUT OF BOUNDS
OFF LIMITS

IT IS STRICTLY FORBIDDEN TO REMOVE STONE OR
ANY OTHER MATERIAL FROM THIS SITE

SOUVENIR HUNTING, WRITING ON WALLS OR
DAMAGE IN ANY FORM WILL BE DEALT WITH AS

MILITARY OFFENCES

DWIGHT D. EISENHOWER,
GENERAL,
Supreme Commander,
Allied Expeditionary Force

By order of
J. E. DIXON-SPAIN
Sqdn Ldr.,
MFA - A. Spec. offr.

Guarding Ancient History

An American soldier guards early Greek temples at Paestum, Italy, which date to around 540 BCE.

OPPOSITE

An early "out of bounds" posting used by MFAA officers in Italy and elsewhere.

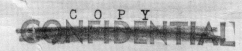

C O P Y

~~CONFIDENTIAL~~

ALLIED FORCE HEADQUARTERS

Office of The Commander-in-Chief

AG 000.4-1

29 December 1943

SUBJECT: Historical Monuments

TO : All Commanders

Today we are fighting in a country which has contributed a great deal to our cultural inheritance, a country rich in monuments which by their creation helped and now in their old age illustrate the growth of the civilization which is ours. We are bound to respect those monuments so far as war allows.

If we have to choose between destroying a famous building and sacrificing our own men, then our men's lives count infinitely more and the buildings must go. But the choice is not always so clear-cut as that. In many cases the monuments can be spared without any detriment to operational needs. Nothing can stand against the argument of military necessity. That is an accepted principle. But the phrase "military necessity" is sometimes used where it would be more truthful to speak of military convenience or even of personal convenience. I do not want it to cloak slackness or indifference.

It is a responsibility of higher commanders to determine through A.M.G. Officers the locations of historical monuments whether they be immediately ahead of our front lines or in areas occupied by us. This information passed to lower echelons through normal channels places the responsibility on all Commanders of complying with the spirit of this letter.

/s/ Dwight D. Eisenhower

DWIGHT D. EISENHOWER,
General, U. S. Army,
Commander-in-Chief.

DISTRIBUTION:
"C"

CLASSIFICATION CHANGED
TO ~~RESTRICTED~~
By authority of CALA
By J. P. PAISLEY
Major. AGD
Date 4 AUG 1945

Restricted Classification
Removed Per
Executive Order 10501

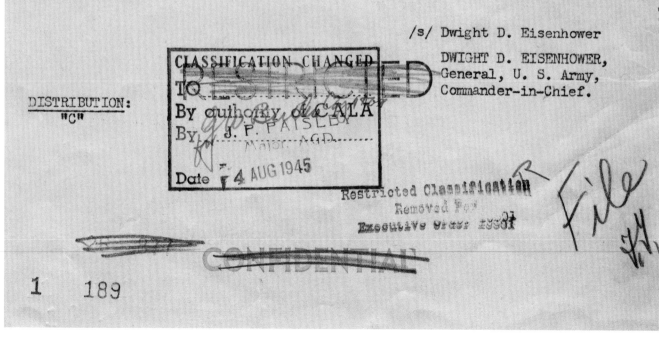

1   189

The Allied Commander-In-Chief General Eisenhower communicated to commanders the importance of respecting monuments and artworks when at all possible.
December 1943

Acerno, Italy
Pvt Paul Oglesby of the
30th Infantry Regiment
pauses to observe this
severely damaged
church. This was an all
too common scence
throughout Italy.
September 1943

SUPREME HEADQUARTERS
ALLIED EXPEDITIONARY FORCE

September, 1944

SUBJECT: Protection of Historical Monuments.

TO   : All Commanders.

1. The Monuments and other Buildings and Sites listed in
this Official List within the area of the responsibility of the
Supreme Commander in Germany are of such cultural importance
that they will not be put to military use without the explicit
permission in each case of the Commanding Generals/Commanders of
Army Groups or of the Commanders to whom they may delegate the
power to give such permission.

2. Commanders will further, at their discretion, protect,
close or put out of bounds to troops any of these monuments,
buildings or sites.

DWIGHT D. EISENHOWER,
General, Commanding.

Distribution "D"

This letter was retyped for C/S

RESTRICTED

SUPREME HEADQUARTERS
ALLIED EXPEDITIONARY FORCE

AG 014.1-1 (Germany) GAP-AGM

C.A.O.'S. OFFICE
22 NOV 1944
Serial No. ....1997........
File ....

APO 757 (Main)
21 November 1944

SUBJECT: Prohibition of Sale and Export of Works of Art in Germany

TO   : All Concerned

Law 52, Article II, paragraph 3 (d) of Proclamations, Laws and
Ordinances, published in connection with the Military Government of Germany,
forbids the sale, transfer and export of works of art and other cultural
material. Its purpose is to make possible the restoration to their rightful
owners of loot taken from other countries. In furtherance of this purpose,
personnel of the Allied Expeditionary Forces in occupied German territory will
not purchase or otherwise traffic in such objects.

By command of General EISENHOWER:

T. J. DAVIS
Brigadier General, USA
Adjutant General

DISTRIBUTION:
"D"

1   18   - 1 -

RESTRICTED

Letters in late 1944 from Gen. Eisenhower and
Brig. Gen. Davis to all commanders
reemphasizing the importance of respecting "no
billeting" postings and, in the case of Brig. Gen.
Davis, a reminder of the prohibition of any
transfer or sale of artworks in occupied German
territory.

OPPOSITE

Aachen

U.S. troops examine the main altar and wreckage inside Aachen Cathedral. It was
damaged during the bitter fighting for the city, which fell to the troops of the U.S. 1st
Army. Aachen was the first significant German city to fall to the Allies.
October 1944

HEADQUARTERS TWELFTH ARMY GROUP
APO 655

386 (G-1)   14 February 1945

SUBJECT: Protection of Property Belonging to Allied Nationals.

TO   : Individual letters to each of the following addressees:

            Commanding General, First US Army, APO 230
            Commanding General, Third US Army, APO 403
            Commanding General, Ninth US Army, APO 339,
            Commanding General, Fifteenth US Army, APO 408
            Commanding General, 66th Infantry Division, APO 454
            Commanding General, Special Troops, Twelfth Army
                                    Group, APO 655.

    1. I have recently been hearing about incidents that have
occurred in which Allied troops have been careless in their manner
of treating property belonging to Allied nationals. I n some
cases buildings have burned down because troops left the buildings
without extinguishing fires. In other cases private property owned
by our Allies has been wantonly destroyed and pillaged.

    2. We are/a conquering army, but we are not a pillaging army.
We do not destroy property unless the enemy forces us to do so.
When our men perform such acts in liberated countries it gives
rise to adverse public opinion. I regret that private property
which was not destroyed during the German occupation should suffer
as a result of undisciplined acts of troops who are members of the
liberating army.

    3. Prevention of such acts lies in discipline and control of
your men. I desire that you give this matter your immediate and
continuing attention.

                            O. N. BRADLEY
                            Lieutenant General U. S. Army
                            Commanding

8   0727

FILE NO. 250

In a memo to other commanding generals, Lt. Gen. Omar Bradley points out, "We are a conquering army…not a pillaging army".

OPPOSITE

Namur
One of the primary roles of Monuments Men was to advise and assist local authorities on the repair and preservation of historical monuments that had suffered damage in war action. In this photograph, Belgian workers repair damage to the windows of the church of Notre Dame in Namur, Belgium, while Monuments officer Lt. Daniel J. Kern supervises the work from a ladder.
Summer 1945

During the Battle of the Bulge, the church in La Gleize, Belgium, was severely damaged. Visible in the shadows of the photograph at left is the statue known as the *Madonna of La Gleize* (above), fully exposed to one of the harshest winters on record. MFAA officer Capt. Walker Hancock aided townspeople in relocating it to a more secure place.
SEE ALSO PAGE 126.

Valogne, France

The Church of St. Malo was unintentionally wrecked by Allied artillery and aerial bombing as part of the pre-landing bombardment to drive German soldiers from the area. This was one of the first opportunities for the Allied Civil Affairs Division to assign work to the handful of Monuments Men then on the ground in Western Europe.

Mr. Rene Jevavasseur (second from left in the photograph at right), an architect from Cherbourg charged by the French Government with the care of historical structures in this region, works with French workers and an American GI to help recover stone carvings, inscriptions and other relics in the rubble of this 13th-century church.
Summer 1944

1. Palazzo Pandolfini
2. Chiosto Dello Scalzo
3. + + Cenalco Di. S. Apollania
4. + + Church and Monastary of S. Marco
5. + R. Biblioteca Marucelliana
6. + + Galleria Dell'Accademia
7. S.S. Annunziata
8. + + + S. Maria Novella
9. + + + S. Lorenzo Laurenziana
10. + + Palazzo Medici
    + R. Biblioteca Riccardiana
11. + + Spedale Degli Innocenti
12. + + Museo Archaeologico
13. + Ognissanti
14. S. Maria Maggiore
15. Archivio Arcivescovile
16. + + + Battistero (Baptistry)
17. + + + Duomo (Cathedral)
18. + Museo Dell'Opera del Duomo
19. S. Maria Nuova
20. S. Maria Madalena Dei Pazzi
21. Loggia Del Bigallo
22. + + Campanile
23. + Museo Nazionale DiAnthropolgia Ed
    Etnologia
24. S. Ambrogio
25. Ponte Alla Carraia
26. Galleria Corsini
27. + + Palazzo Rucellai
28. + + Palazzo Strozzi
29. Palazzo Davanzanti
30. + + Or San Michele Palazzo Dell'Arte
    Della Lana
31. Badia
32. + + + Palazzo Della Podesta
    + + + Museo Nazionale
33. S. Simone
34. + + Casa Buonarroti
35. + + S. Trinita
36. Palazzo Bartonlini Salimbeni
37. Palazzo Di Parte Guelfa
38. Palazzo Gondi
39. + + S.S. Apostoli
40. + Loggia Dei Lanzi
41. + + + Palazzo Vecchio
    + + Archivo Storico Del Comune
42. + + + S. Maria Del Carmine
43. + + + S. Spirito
44. Palazzo Capponi
45. Ponte S. Trinita
46. Ponte Vecchio
47. + + + Palazzo Degli Uffizi
48. Museo Delle Scienze
49. + Museo Horne
50. + + + R. Biblioteca Nazionale Centrale
    + + + S. Croce Museo Dell' Opera Di S.
    Croce
51. Palazzo Gudagni
52. S. Felicita
53. S. Felice
54. + + + Palazzo Pitti & Boboli Gardens
55. + Museo Bardini
56. S. NIccolo Sopr' Arno
57. S. Salvatore Al Monte
58. + + S. Miniato Al Monte

MFAA officials used an aerial photograph of Florence to prepare an extensively detailed and precise legend identifying cultural treasures of varying importance. These famous monuments had to be avoided by pilots on their bombing run to knock out the Campo di Marte rail yard, an important military transit point being used by German forces to move arms and munitions. The last of two bombing runs occured on March 23, 1944, by the 42nd Wing of the U.S. Army Air Force, with extremely accurate results. Virtually all of the 160 bombs hit their target.

The Roberts Commission Report, prepared in 1946, included a list of those who served in the MFAA section. To the best of our knowledge, this list was never updated to include the numerous others who had active roles in the protection and restitution of Europe's artistic heritage and those who served in the Far Eastern Theater of Operations. We have thus supplemented the Roberts Commission list with the names of others mentioned in books and articles written by key MFAA personnel as well as compiled names from other lists subsequently generated by government officials.

Adams, Capt. Edward E.

Albright, Lt. Frank P.

Amand, Marcel

Anderson, Maj. Harry A.

Apgar, T/Sgt. Horace

Appel, S/Sgt. William B.

Archey, Gilbert

Armstrong, S/Sgt. Robert G.

Arnold, John G.

Baillie-Reynolds, Maj. P. K.

Balfour, Maj. Ronald E.

Barancik, Pfc. Richard M.

Baudouin, Frans

Beaufort, René

Bell, Maj. H.E.

Bencowitz, Isaac

Bernholz, Charles

Bilodeau, Pfc. Francis W.

Bleecker, Pfc. Paul O.

Boardman, Lt. Edward T.

Boell, Jesse E.

Bonilla, Felix

Bonzom, Eugene

Boon, K. G.

Born, Maj. Lester K.

Boruch, T/4 Edward J.

Bovio, Flora

Bowie, Mrs. Barbara H.

Bradford, Capt. John S.P.

Breitenbach, Edgar, E & C.R. DIV.

Broerman, Paul

Bromwich, Maj. John

Brooke, Capt. T. Humphrey

Brown, John Nicholas

Bryant, Capt. William C.

Brye, Hubert de

Buchman, Capt. Julius H.

Buckingham, Pfc. Russell H.

Bumbar, Lt. Julianna

Burks, Capt. Bernard D.

Busey, Capt. C.

Callon, Margaret

Carr, Allan

Casson, Lt. Col. S.

Chadwick, Cpl. Gordon

Chance, Capt. R.

Charles, Rollo

Cheguillaume, M. J.

Chevigny, Prince

Child, Sgt. Burrage Christopher

Clarke, Lt. Roger A.

Clem, Harold J. Pol. Aff. Div.

Conrad, Lt. Doda

Cook, J. M.

Cook, S/Sgt. James O.

Cooper, Douglas

Coremans, Paul B.

Corrigan, Sgt. Gordon F.

Cott, Lt. Cdr. Perry B. USNR

Coulter, Lt. Cdr. Hamilton USNR

Croft-Murray, Capt. E.

Davie, L.G.

Davis, Cpl. Clyde I

Davis, Lt. Richard S. USNR

Dawson, Capt. Eric A.

de Beer

Defino, S/Sgt. L.

Delsaux

de Villeret

Devinna, Maurice A., Jr.

DeWald, Lt. Col. Ernest T.

Dewitt, Maj. Roscoe P.

Dierkauf

Dignam, Celia

Diraimondo, T/4 Charles J.

Dixon-Spain, Sqdr. Ldr. J.E.

Dlugosz, T/4 Louis F.

Doane, Capt. Gilbert R.

Dollfus

Doman, Andrea

Donn, D.L.,

Doubinsky, Elie J. B.

Downey, Lt. Glanville

Dreyfus, Carle

Druene

Duchartre, P. L.

Dunbabin, T. J.

Eden, Peter

Ellis, Capt. R. H.

Enthoven, Capt. Roedrick E.

Ermatinger, T/4 Charles J.

Estreicher, Karol

Ettlinger, T/5 Harry L.

Faison, Lt. Cdr. S. Lane

Farmer, Capt. Walter I.

Fleetwood-Hesketh, P.

Fleischner, Charles

Florisoone, Michel

Ford, Lt. Dale V.

France, Capt. Leys A.

Francois, Michel

French, T. W.

Fujishiro, Motoko

Fuller, Capt. A.

Gabriel, Pfc. Richard F.

Gallagher, Charles F.

Gangnat, Philippe

Gardner, Lt. Col. Paul

Gear, William

Giuli, Capt. Thomas

Glass, Robert

Goldberg, T/5 S. L.

Goodison, John W.

Gould, Capt. Cecil

Granger-Taylor, Jerry, Elysium

Granswickel, Jr., Dr. Dirk P. M.

Grier, Capt. Harry D.

Grinbarg, Lt. Morrie S.

Hald, Pfc. William

Halsall, Capt.

Hammett, Capt. Ralph W.

Hammon, Maj. Stratton

Hammond, Lt. Col. Mason

Hammond, Lt. Col. N. C. L.

Hancock, Capt. Walker K.

Hansen, T/4 Robert W.

Harboard, Felix

Harris, Lt. Clyde K.

Hartigan, Maj. John D.

Hartt, Lt. Frederick

Harvey, John

Hathaway, Capt. Calvin S.

Hauschildt. Lt. Kurt F.

Haynes, Denys E. L.

Hayward, John F.

Heinrich, Lt. Theodore A.

Henderson, Harold G.

Henraux, A. S.

Henry, T/5 Alfred

Hensley, Maj. Richard G.

Higgins, Stephen

Hocart, Raymond

Holland, Eleanor S.

Hollis, Howard C.

Horn, Lt. Walter W.

Horne, J. Anthony

Howard, Richard F.

Howe, Lt. Cdr. Tom Jr.

Huberman, Pfc. Harry

Huchthausen, Capt. Walter J.

Hugoboom

Hutchinson, Lucy

Hyslop, Capt. G.,

Jacka, Pauline

Jaffe, Hans C. L.

Jaujard, Jacques

Jefferson, Col.

Jenkinson, Sir Hilary C.B.E.

Jennings, Pfc. R. J.

Johnson, Sgt. Lorin K.

Kates, George N.,

Kavli, Capt. Guthorm

Keck, Lt. Sheldon W.

Keezer, Marcellus B.

Kelleher, Capt. Patrick J.

Keller, Capt. Deane

Kern, Lt. Daniel J.

Keyes, James H.

King, Donald

Kinzie, Capt. Joseph R.

Kirstein, Pfc. Lincoln E.

Koberstein, T/4 Freeman G.

Koch, Lt. Albert C. USNR

Koch, Lt. Robert A.

Kormendi, S/Sgt. Andre

Kovalyak, Lt. Stephen

Kuhlke, Lt. Richard H.

Kuhn, Lt. Cdr. Charles L.

La Boulaye, Paul de.

Lacey, Capt. George T.

LaFarge, Capt. Bancel

Langui, Emile

Lardner, Cpl. W. C.

A Capt. Frederick Hartt, world-renowned historian of Italian art, poses next to his jeep with an unidentified artifact.
Livorno, Italy 1944

B Capt. Deane Keller examines a portion of the damaged structure of Campo Santo in Pisa.
Summer 1945

C Lt. Col. Ernest DeWald (left) and Capt. R. H. Ellis, begin the nearly impossible task of recovering the priceless archives of the medieval Abbey of Monte Cassino, which had been largely destroyed in a long and bloody battle between Allied and German forces.
1944

D Louvre curator, Major René Huyghe (standing, second from left) poses with his Resistance troops who assisted in the wartime safeguarding of France's cultural treasures against the Nazi occupiers.
Summer 1944

E Lt. James Rorimer (kneeling, at left) and Louvre curator Germain Bazin pose in front of Goya's painting, *Time*, which had been successfully protected during the war at Château de Sourches.
August 1944

A Monuments Men and Louvre officials, including curator Bazin (middle), pause for a photograph during their efforts to secure and return France's safeguarded treasures.
Paris 1944

B Dutch art official, Lt. Col. Alphonse Vorenkamp (center) with Lt. Cdr. Hamilton Coulter (right) and curatorial assistant Birkmeyer on the morning of a restitution shipment to the Netherlands.
Munich Collecting Point 1945

C Polish art officer and hero, Capt. Karol Estreicher (second from left), stands in front of one of the famous Bellotto paintings looted from the Warsaw Castle. German art expert Dr. Hans Röthel (left) stands next to MFAA officer Dr. Edgar Breitenbach (center), acting director of the Collecting Point after Craig Smyth's departure in March 1946. Erika Hanfstaengl, an art assistant at the Collecting Point, is at right.
Munich Collecting Point

D Capt. Walker Hancock, Capt. Asa M. Thornton, and Lt. Cdr. George Stout pose at an unidentified location.
1944

A Lt. Col. Mason Hammond (left), a distinguished Classics Professor at Harvard, and Lt. James Rorimer, future Director of the Metropolitan Museum of Art in New York, help recover works hidden in the Kochendorf-Heilbronn mines.
Heilbronn, Germany July 1945

B Civilian Advisor to the MFAA, Dr. Andrew Ritchie, a future Director at both the Museum of Modern Art in New York and the Yale University Art Gallery.
Munich Collecting Point

C Capt. Seymour Pomrenze (center), Director of the Offenbach Collecting Point, with French officials Lt. Col. Jean Prinet (left) and Cdr. Ph. Gangnat (right).
Offenbach Collecting Point

D The effects of war are distinctly visible in the gaunt figure of Dr. Otto Kümmel, one of Hitler's main art strategists and author of the notorious "shopping list" of masterpieces to be stolen from countries as they were occupied by German troops. He is seen here, after his capture, with Capt. Calvin Hathaway (right).
Germany July 1945

E Officers of the Art Looting Investigation Unit (ALIU) of the Office of Strategic Services (OSS), precursor to the Central Intelligence Agency (CIA): Theodore Rousseau and James Plaut at the interrogation center in Alt Aussee.
Alt Aussee, Austria 1945

A Lt. Cdr. Thomas Carr Howe, Jr., the director of the Legion of Honor Museum, San Francisco, before and after the war.
Alt Aussee 1945

B Lt. Lamont Moore, a fine arts scholar and future associate at Yale University Art Gallery.
Alt Aussee July1945

C Lt. Cdr. S. Lane Faison, Jr., also a member of the Art Looting Investigation Unit (ALIU), and Professor of Art at Williams College, Massachusetts.
1943

D Lt. Dale V. Ford was in charge of recovery efforts at the twin Kochendorf and Heilbronn mines in Germany. He was later President of the David Wolcott Kendall Memorial School, a school of design that is now part of Ferris State University in Grand Rapids, Michigan.
Germany 1946

E Sgt. Harry L. Ettlinger, a Jewish refugee, fled to the United States from Germany in 1938. In 1944, he joined the U.S. Army and returned to Europe as an infantryman. On his ninteenth birthday, he was pulled from combat to be used as an interpreter. At the end of the war, he volunteered to work for then Capt. James Rorimer, heading the 7th Army MFAA. His first assignment was to interview the infamous Heinrich Hoffmann, Hitler's personal photographer. He also helped supervise recovery efforts at Heilbronn with Lt. Ford, where one of his important tasks was the packing and return of the stained glass windows from Strasbourg Cathedral.
Germany 1946

F Sgt. Kenneth C. Lindsay poses with the priceless Bust of Queen Nefertiti, an ancient Egyptian sculpture from the Egyptian Museum in Berlin. He worked under Capt. Farmer at the Weisbaden Collecting Point and was later a Professor of Art at the State University of New York in Binghamton.
Wiesbaden Collecting Point

A Capt. Walter I. Farmer, Director of the Wiesbaden Collecting Point and a designer and architect by trade, discusses a painting with an associate. The men are surrounded by priceless works of Italian art.
Wiesbaden Collecting Point

B Lt. Col. Geoffrey Webb, a British officer and chief MFAA advisor to Gen. Eisenhower, played a critical leadership role in helping to salvage cultural treasures in France and Germany.
1945

C Lt. Col. J. B. Ward Perkins, another important British Monuments Man, was Deputy Director of the MFAA Sub-commission headquarters in Italy.
January 1945

D Bernard Taper, Art Intelligence officer with the MFAA in Germany, was responsible for tracking down countless lost masterpieces. He was a journalism professor at the University of California, Berkeley, and also wrote for *The New Yorker* and a number of other publications.
1946

E Pfc. Lincoln Kirstein participated in several of the most significant discoveries of hidden art, none larger than that of Alt Aussee. After the war he was the founder of what would become the New York City Ballet.

F Capt. Edith Standen and Louvre official Rose Valland examine part of a Rodin sculpture before its return to France.
Wiesbaden Collecting Point

A Rose Valland, French heroine of World War II, receives one of many awards for her courageous deeds during the German occupation. Valland, a French museum official whom the Nazis allowed to work in the Jeu de Paume, secretly maintained records of countless looted artworks so that they could be located and recovered after the war.

B A group of Allied art officers, from left to right, back row: Lt. Col. Carlton Harris, John Nicholas Brown, Lt. Col. Lawrence P. Sangston, Major Dittenhofer, and Capt. Bruce Reagan; front row: Major Mason Hammond, Lt. Kenneth Lippman, Lt. Calvin Hathaway, and Lt. Harry K. Waymoth.
Bushy Park, England March 1945

C This group gathered to witness the return to Belgium of Michelangelo's *Bruges Madonna*. Standing, from left to right: Lt. Col. Ernest DeWald, MFAA officer in Austria; Emile Langui, Belgian official; Capt. Steven Kovalyak, U.S. Army; Lt. Craig Hugh Smyth; Dr. Andrew Ritchie, civilian advisor to the MFAA in Munich; Cdr. George Boas, U.S. Naval Attaché, U.S. Embassy in Belgium; Maj. Bancel LaFarge, senior MFAA officer with the U.S. 12th Army.
Munich Collecting Point 1945

D Left to right: Capt. Marcelle Minet, France; Lt. Craig Hugh Smyth; Capt. Hubert de Brye, France (above); Lt. Col. Alphonse Vorenkamp, the Netherlands (below); Lt. Doda Conrad; Lt. Jean Lemaire, Belgium; Lt. Charles Parkhurst; and Maj. Pierre Duchartre, France.
Munich Collecting Point 1945

The Home Front: Safeguarding Europe's Cultural Patrimony from Afar

A Dr. Paul J. Sachs, founding member and Chairman of the American Defense—Harvard Group, which successfully lobbied for the creation of the American Commission for the Protection and Salvage of Artistic and Historic Monuments in War Areas. A member of the Roberts Commission, Dr. Sachs was also a distinguished Professor of Fine Arts and Associate Director of the Fogg Art Museum at Harvard University.

B Dr. William Bell Dinsmoor and Dr. Sumner McKnight Crosby, the respective Chairman and Executive Secretary of the American Council of Learned Societies, discuss a U.S. Army Air Force aerial photograph of the principal cultural treasures of Pisa.

C Dr. Francis Henry Taylor, Vice-Chairman of the Roberts Commission (American Commission for the Protection and Salvage of Artistic and Historic Monuments in War Areas), and Director of the Metropolitan Museum of Art in New York.

D Supreme Court Justice Owen J. Roberts, Chairman of the American Commission for the Protection and Salvage of Artistic and Historic Monuments In War Areas.

E Supreme Court Chief Justice Harlan F. Stone, advisory member of the Roberts Commission.

Larwood, Capt. James B.

Lazareff, Professor Victor

Lee, Sherman E.

Lehmann-Haupt, Hellmut

Lemaire, Raymond

Leonard, Hebert

Lesley, Capt. Everett P.

Lewis

Lindsay, Sgt. Kenneth C.

Lovegrove, Lt. William A.

Lucia, Sgt. A. P.

Maehler, Pvt. Wolfgang

Markham, Maj. S. F.

Markus, Pvt. Werner

Marriott, Capt. Basil

Marteau

Mast

Maxse, Capt. Fred, H.J.

McCain, Capt. William D.

McDonnell, Lt. Col. A. J. L.

McDowall, E.

McGinn, T/5 Elizabeth A.

Mitchell, Capt. Charles

Monroe, Robert

Moore, Lt. Lamont

Morey, Capt. Jonathan T.

Mull, Jane, Fortune

Munby, A. N. L.

Munich, Canada

Munsing, Stefan P.

Murray-Baillie, Capt. Hughe

Mutrux, Capt. E. J.

Myers, T/5 Denys P.

Newton, Col. Henry C.

Newton, Maj. Norman

Nicholls, Capt. John F.

Norins, Capt. Leslie H.

Norris, E. Christopher

Ossorio, Frederic E.

Parkhurst, Lt. Charles P. USNR

Pascale, Cpl. D.

Peck, Edward S.

Peebles, S/Sgt. Bernard M.

Pennoyer, Capt. A. Sheldon

Perkins, Lt. Col. J. B. Ward

Perry, Maj. Lionel

Phillips, Cpl. John M.

Phillips, Ewan

Pilliod, Henri E.

Pinsent, Capt. C. R.

Pinsent, Cecil R.

Plaut, Lt. Cdr. J. S. USNR

Pleasants, Frederick R.

Plumer, James Marshall

Pomrenze, Capt. Seymour J.

Popham, Anne

Popham, Capt. Walter D.

Posey, Capt. Robert K.

Poste, Lt. Leslie I.

Potts, Georgiana

Preston, T/Sgt. Stuart

Prinet, Jean

Prochaska, Pvt. Ladislav L.

Propst, Capt. Kenneth H.

Puyvelde, Len van

Rae, Capt. Edwin C.

Ratensky, Lt. Samuel

Robertson, Maj. G. H.

Roell, D.C.

Rogin, Lt. Martin

Rorimer, Capt. James J.

Ross, Capt. Marvin C. USMCR

Ross, Maj. Malcolm

Ross, Michael

Rousseau, Theodore, Jr.

Rouvier, Jean

Sage, Lt. R. W.

Sakin, Eugene

Sampson, T/5 Selena WAC

Sanchez, Manuel

Sattgast, Capt. Charles R.

Sawyer, Pfc. Charles H.

Scarff, John Henry

Scarpitta, S.C., Jr.

Schmidt, S/Sgt. Gerlot W.

Schoonbrood, Jack

Selke, Maj. George

Shepherd, Dorothy G.

Shipman, Fred W.

Shrady, Lt. Frederick C.

Sickman, Lawrence W. R.

Sickman, Maj. Laurence

Sizer, Maj. Theodore

Skelton, Dorothy G.S.

Skelton, R. A.

Skilton, Lt. John D., Jr.

Smyth, Lt. Craig H. USNR

Sponenburgh, Capt. Mark R.

Stach, Jochem

Standen, Capt. Edith A.

Steer, Capt. Kenneth

Steiner, Lt. Walter

Stopek, T/5 Harry

Stout, Lt. Cdr. George L. USNR

Stroell, Miss Barbara

Taper, Bernard

Taylor, Capt.

Taylor, Mrs. Katharie W. W.

Thornton, Capt. Asa M.

Tregor, Capt. Nison A.

Tucker, Eve

Valland, Rose

Van Der Haut, Hendrik

Van Nisse, Verschoor

Van Nortwick, Capt. William B.

Vanderbilt, Paul

Vanuxem, Jacques

Vlug

Vorenkamp, Alphonse

Vrecko, Frant

Vries, Dr. A. B. de

Vroom, Dr. N. R. A.

Wagstaff, Capt. G. F. T.

Walker, Cpl. William

Walsh

Ward Perkins, Lt. Col. J.B.

Warner, Langdon

Waterhouse, Maj. Ellis K.

Watson, Hon. Mark

Waugh, Capt. Sidney

Webb, Col. Geoffrey F.

Westland, Althea

Whatmough, S/Sgt. J. N.

Wijsenbeek, L. J. F.

Wilkes, Lt. David G.

Willard, Cpl. Edward N.

Willess, T/5 Lester M.

Williams, Maj. Lewis S.

Willmot, Maj. G. F.

Winkler, Dr. Erik

Wittman, Maj. Otto

Wolff, Mme.

Woolley, Lt. Col. Sir Leonard

Yoda, Takayoshi

Young, Capt. David K.

Yuill Maj. Ralph W.

Zimmermann, Lt. J. E.

VOLUNTEER ASSISTANTS

Avery, Myrtilla

Banister, Turpin

Bonfante, Julian

Bromberg, Paul

Day, John

de Tolnay, Charles

Delmar, Emil

Dinsmoor, Mrs. Zillah P.

Frankl, Paul

Giedion, Siegfried

Goodrich, L.C.

Graves, Mortimer

Hall, Lindsley

Hauser, Walter

Ingholt, Harald

Jayne, Horace H.F.

Kelemen, Pal

Levi della Vida, Giorgio

Levi, Doro

Lugt, Frits

Manning, Clarence A.

Mayer, A. Hyatt

Meiss, Millard

Menzies, James

Meyer, Jose

Munzer, Mrs. Zdenka

Paine, Robert T., Jr.

Panofsky, Erwin

Philippart, Georges

Priest, Alan

Reinhart, Anita

Richter, Gisela M. A.

Rowland, Benjamin, Jr.

Salmony, Alfred

Schönberger, Guido

Schuster, Carl

Sterling, Charles

Stuart, Meriwether

Swift, Emerson H.

Thimme, Dieter

Tietze, Hans

Tietze, Mrs. Hans

Venturi, Lionello

Weinberger, Martin

Weitzmann, Kurt

Weitzmann-Fiedler, Josefa

Wenley, A.G.

White, William C.

Wilkinson, Charles

"It [Major Balfour's death] is a great and unexpected blow. He had written only the day before, so cheerfully, delighted with being at the front; then he was killed in action, where actually engaged in saving some of those works of art which he loved so much. He had done wonderfully good work, as those who knew him knew he would do; he leaves a gap in our service which no one will be able to fill so well. The whole field of art history has suffered a tragic loss."

—LT. COL. SIR LEONARD WOOLLEY, BRITISH MFAA OFFICER, ADVISOR TO THE WAR OFFICE, LONDON

Major Ronald Edmund Balfour, K.R.R.C.

British Monuments, Fine Arts, and Archives officer with the 2nd Canadian Army. Born in England in 1904, Major Balfour was killed in action while rescuing cultural treasures in Clèves, Germany, on March 10, 1945. He was a historian and Fellow at King's College, Cambridge, to which he left his entire personal library of 8000 books.

Major Balfour's last report, filed March 3, 1945, described his work in the Stiftskirche (church) in Clèves: "Fragments of two large 16th century retables [altarpieces] of carved and painted wood have been collected and removed to safety. Parish archives found in a blasted safe and strewn over the floor of the wrecked sacristy have also been removed for safe-keeping."

One week later, on March 10, as Major Balfour and four other men were moving sculpture from Christ the King Church down Kellen road in Clèves, the only shell to fall on the city that day landed in the road next to them. Balfour, who was alone on one side of the street, was the sole casualty.

"The American Commission has learned with the deepest regret of the death of your son Captain Walter Huchthausen. Captain Huchthausen was, in the opinion of this Commission, one of the outstanding Monuments Officers in the field, and his work in the Valley of the Loire and at Aachen will remain as a signal contribution to the cultural preservation of Europe. His knowledge of Germany made him uniquely fitted for the work there and his loss is an irreparable one."

—David E. Finley, Chairman of the Roberts Commission (American Commission for the Protection and Salvage of Artistic and Historic Monuments in War Areas) and future Director of the National Gallery of Art, Washington, D.C.

Captain Walter Johan Huchthausen
U.S. Monuments, Fine Arts, and Archives Officer with the U.S. 9th Army in France and Germany. Born in Perry, Oklahoma on December 19, 1904, Captain Huchthausen was killed in action while rescuing cultural treasures in Germany, in April 1945. Educated at the University of Minnesota and Harvard University, where he earned a Master of Architecture degree in 1930, Huchthausen taught at the Rensselaer Polytechnic Institute in Troy, New York, and the Boston Museum School of Fine Arts, where he was director of the Department of Design in 1935-39, and finally at the University of Minnesota until his military enlistment in 1942. He served admirably with the MFAA in the Loire Valley, France, and in Germany, particularly in the heavily-damaged town of Aachen.

TREASURE FOUND

"We followed him [the miner] into the unlighted mine chamber. Flashlights supplemented the wavering flames of the miner's lamps. Ahead of us we could make out row after row of high packing cases. Beyond them was a broad wooden platform. The rays of our flashlights revealed a bulky object resting on the center of the platform. We came closer. We could see that it was a statue, a marble statue, and then we knew—it was Michelangelo's Madonna from Bruges, one of the world's great masterpieces."

LT. CDR. THOMAS CARR HOWE, JR., USNR
MONUMENTS, FINE ARTS, AND ARCHIVES OFFICER

For even the most experienced museum curator or art historian, much less the average soldier, the experience of discovering some of the world's most famous and valuable works of art was both unimaginable and overwhelming. Wars inevitably give rise to bizarre scenes of familiar objects in incongruous settings: museum collections found unprotected in railcars; fragile paintings and sculpture stacked on the ground or leaning against the dank walls of salt mines; and religious relics and ancient books strewn thick across the floors of buildings and warehouses. Such were a few of the circumstances in which the treasures of Western civilization were found by MFAA officers.

In Italy, paintings taken from museums in Naples and Florence, which had been placed for safekeeping at repositories in nearby villas, were missing. They were last seen in the possession of retreating German troops. Continuing Allied military success provided access to northern Italy and led to the subsequent discovery by MFAA officers of most of the stolen works of art from these museums and others in Italy.

In France, Rose Valland's detailed information on ERR theft operations at the Jeu de Paume in Paris directed MFAA officers to a remote castle in Neuschwanstein, Germany. In May, 1945, they would find not just stolen art and furniture from the

Piles of boxes, records, and clothing are guarded by an American GI inside a church in Ellingen, Germany. The church had been used by the Nazis as a secret depot for clothing requisitioned from France and Holland.
April 26, 1945

collections of prominent French collectors such as the Rothschild family, but also the ERR card catalogues and records. These records greatly aided MFAA officers in their recovery efforts and, in particular, the return of stolen works to their owners. Even then, it took more than a year to identify and remove all the looted works, many of which were still in the unopened crates used by the ERR when they were shipped from Paris.

While the value of paintings and other art objects was not always evident to military personnel, hoards of cash, gold, and diamonds needed little explanation. Discovery of the Merkers mine in Germany by advance troops from General George S. Patton's Third Army Group was comparable to finding the contents of Fort Knox in a remote unguarded cave. Because news of a find of this magnitude spread quickly, troops became excited—even eager—to be the next ones to find buried treasure. With its discovery, the hunt in Germany for other troves began in earnest.

The largest and most important discovery of stolen artworks was that of Alt Aussee, Austria, in a salt mine located about fifty miles southeast of Salzburg. More than one mile into the mountain, in a series of interwoven tunnels, Monuments Men discovered more than 6,500 paintings. Many were destined for the museums Hitler had planned for Linz and other Austrian cities. There were thousands of drawings, pieces of sculpture, and books, as well as hundreds of boxes and baskets with unknown contents. Included were the missing paintings from Naples which

had been stolen by officers of the Hermann Göring Tank Division as a gift for their leader. It took more than three months for MFAA officers to empty the mine. The quality was staggering: Two paintings by Vermeer, a sculpture by Michelangelo, one of the world's greatest altarpieces, painted by Van Eyck, and hundreds of other unique treasures which had been placed in storage awaiting safe passage to the walls of Hitler's obsession: The Führer Museum in Linz.

Over the next few years more than a thousand hiding places were discovered by Allied forces, often times the result of a tip garnered from area residents. Each time a new repository was found, the same procedure was followed: the site was secured and its contents were inventoried. The Monuments Men had to scrounge up materials that would suffice for packing supplies, find transportation vehicles and drivers, and then remove the contents item by item for relocation to one of several Collecting Points. This process usually took months and, in a few instances, more than a year. Wartime shortages meant seemingly simple day-to-day items weren't available. Road conditions were usually hazardous, sometimes harrowingly so due to the mountainous location of mines such as Alt Aussee in the Austrian Alps. That whole truckloads of paintings were not damaged by potholes and bomb craters in the road or destroyed because of trucks careening off the side of a road serves as a testament to the determination and responsibility shared by Monuments Men. Innovation, hardwork, and a little luck were their constant companions.

The villa of Montegufoni, outside Florence, where many works of art from Florentine museums were stored. Montegufoni was one of several privately owned villas outside Florence used by art officials to store paintings from the Uffizi Gallery and other Florentine museums.

U.S. officers from 5th Army are leaving the Dornsberg Castle in northern Italy, in search of loot hidden by German soldiers. Large quantities of silk, wool and other stolen goods were found in the castle.

TREASURE TROVES

Neuchwanstein

Built by "Mad Ludwig" of Bavaria in the nineteenth century, the castle became a central German depot for art and other items stolen from France.

Alt Aussee

U.S. troops pose in front of the main building of the salt mine at Alt Aussee in Austria. Inside its vast underground complex, the Allies discovered the most important cache of looted art in the war.

May 1945

ITALY

Giotto di Bondone,
Ognissanti Madonna
(Madonna Enthroned with
Child, Angels, and Saints),
1305-10.
Panel, 3.25 × 2.04 m
(10 ft 8 in × 6 ft 8 in).
Uffizi, Florence.

Montegufoni

When Dr. Cesare Fasola, Uffizi librarian, arrived at the villa of Montegufoni to check on the repository, he was appalled to see that many of the cases had been pried open by German troops. Some paintings had been stacked in areas used by soldiers as a latrine. Uffizi paintings included the *Equestrian Portrait of Philip IV of Spain*, attributed to the School of Rubens; to the right is the beautiful *Ognissanti Madonna* by Giotto.

September 1944

Capt. Deane Keller poses with Botticelli's masterpiece, *La Primavera* (see following page), which was successfully protected at Montegufoni.

Sandro Botticelli,
La Primavera, **c. 1482.**
Tempera on panel,
2.03 × 3.14 m
(6 ft 8 in × 10 ft 3 in).
Uffizi, Florence.

Campo Tures
Men of Company K, 339th Infantry Regiment, 85th Inf. Div., look over some of the stolen paintings and sculptures they discovered.
May 1945

Merano
Lt. Col. Ralph E. Haines, Senior Military Commander of Merano, and Dr. Van Hartner, representative of the International Red Cross from Budapest, examine a few of the many expensive rugs looted by German troops from merchants in Milan and Turin. The rugs were stored in the Dornsberg Castle.
May 1945

GERMANY

Ehrenbreitstein
Herr Cornelius Shoss, employed as caretaker
at the Cologne Museum, examines one of the
paintings evacuated for safekeeping to the
historic fortress of Ehrenbreitstein, General
Pershing's headquarters during World War I.
March 1945

Siegen

The copper mine in Siegen temporarily became known as the "Golden Arrow Art Museum" named after the U.S. 8th Army's insignia. As it was the first discovery of a major repository, news spread quickly among other troops.

In the photograph above, U.S. 1st Army Pfc. Tony Baca of Santa Fe, New Mexico, looks at a beautiful painting by Rubens, one of the many valuable works of art discovered in the mine.

In the photograph on the left, an American GI peers into shelves filled with paintings. In the foreground is a wooden Madonna.
April 1945

Grasleben

Some Berlin Museum pictures were transferred to Grasleben, but not until March, 1945. Lt. Lamont Moore reported the discovery of the Schönebeck-Grasleben mine in April, 1945. In the photograph at right British officers examine hundreds of uncrated paintings lying on the stone floor of the mine with no protective covering. In the photograph below, MFAA officers Lts. Lamont Moore and Sheldon Keck inspect looted Polish treasure.

Merkers

In the salt mine at Merkers, Germany, members of the 90th Division, U.S. 3rd Army, discovered a portion of the Reichsbank gold and currency, SS loot, and German museum artworks evacuated from Berlin. In the photograph above, GIs use a jeep and trailer to remove gold from the mine, guarded by a soldier operating a .30 caliber machine gun. In the photograph on the left, two American GIs remove a case of historic engravings from the vault.

April 1945

Hidden inside the Merkers salt mine was the Reichsbank
wealth: Germany's gold reserves and paper currency.
Most all but the largest paintings from the Kaiser-
Friedrich Museum in Berlin were placed there for
safekeeping. Evidence of Nazi atrocities was also present:
gold fillings and other valuables taken from victims of
Hitler's tyranny. The discovery of the mine was made by
the 90th Division of U.S. 3rd Army led by General Patton.

American GIs admire *In the Conservatory*, a masterpiece by Edouard Manet. This painting, from the Kaiser-Friedrich Museum in Berlin, had been brought to the mine for safekeeping.

Edouard Manet, *In the Conservatory*, 1879.
Oil on canvas, 115 × 150 cm (45 ¼ × 59 in).
Gemäldegalerie, Berlin.

Sgt. Harold Mans of Scranton, Pennsylvania, examines a box of woodcut prints by the German Renaissance artist, Albrecht Dürer, which was found in a secret chamber in the mine. He is looking at a print entitled *The Beast with Lamb's Horns* from the artist's famous *Apocalypse* series of 1498.

Gen. Dwight D. Eisenhower, Supreme Allied Commander, inspects art treasures stored in the depths of the mine. Behind General Eisenhower are Lt. Gen. Omar N. Bradley (left), CG, 12th Army Group, and Lt. Gen. George S. Patton, Jr, CG, U.S. 3rd Army (right). This was a momentous and exceedingly challenging day for the three generals. In addition to their trip to Merkers, they also visited one of the first Nazi concentration camps liberated by American forces in Ohrdruf, Germany. The horror so overwhelmed Lt. Gen. Patton that he became sick to his stomach. Later that day came the news of the death of President Roosevelt.
April 12, 1945

Heilbronn

The salt mine in Heilbronn was converted into a bombproof repository for artworks and other looted Nazi treasure stored 500 feet below ground. Among the cache discovered by Allied Forces were many of Germany's finest museum collections that had been evacuated for safekeeping, including paintings from Karlsruhe, Mannheim and Stuttgart.
April 1945

A soldier watches as two mine workers open a crate which contained stained glass removed for safekeeping from the Cathedral in Strasbourg, France. This was one of many treasures Allied Forces discovered in the Heilbronn salt mine.
September 1945

The Strasbourg Cathedral was built over a 300-year period. Early buildings on that site are documented as far back as the eighth century. The Cathedral is a combination of styles of which late-Romanesque and Gothic elements are most prominent. It is renowned for its stained glass windows, some of which are datable to the beginning of the thirteenth century. Many of the stained glass panels depict stories from the Old and New Testaments such as *King Solomon and the Queen of Sheba*, *David and Solomon*, and *Christ Teaching*.

Numerous crates filled with paintings such as these were discovered in the Heilbronn mine.

Lucas Cranach the Elder, *Madonna and Child*, 1518.
Oil on panel, 34.5 × 22.6 cm (13 × 8 ⅞ in). Staatliche Kunsthalle Karlsruhe, Germany.

Lucas Cranach the Elder, *Judgment of Paris*, c. 1515.
Oil on panel, 35 × 24 cm (13 ¾ × 9 ½ in). Staatliche Kunsthalle Karlsruhe, Germany.

Master of the Karlsruhe Passion, *Crucifixion*, from the Passion Series, c. 1450-55.
Oil on panel, 60 × 47 cm (23 ⅝ × 18 ½ in). Staatliche Kunsthalle Karlsruhe, Germany.

Monuments Man Sgt. Harry L. Ettlinger stands amid rows of crated art treasures stolen from the occupied countries of France, Holland, and Belgium. The Heilbronn mine was one of the largest repositories because it also included works from many German museums evacuated for safekeeping. The Viola d'Amour, made in Italy, belongs to the School of Music in Mannheim, Germany.

This *Self Portrait* by Rembrandt, inspected by Lt. Dale V. Ford and Sgt. Ettlinger, was stored for safe-keeping in the Heilbronn mine by museum officials from Karlsruhe. The painting was returned to the museum.

OPPOSITTE

**Rembrandt van Rijn,
Self Portrait, c. 1650.**
Oil on panel (oval),
69 × 56 cm (27 × 22 in).
Staatliche Kunsthalle
Karlsruhe, Germany.

Neuschwanstein Castle

The photograph on the left shows a room of the castle that contains bin after bin of furniture stolen by the ERR, Alfred Rosenberg's task force. Much of it belonged to the Rothschild family in Paris. In the photograph below, two unidentified men stand in a small store room filled with sculpture and other items.
May 1945

"According to this report, 21,903 objects taken from 203 private collections, were removed, notably from the Rothschild, Alphons Kahn, David Weil, Lévy de Benzion, and the Seligmann brothers collections. According to the same report there were 'all told, 29 transports, 137 trucks, and 4,174 cases.'"

WRITTEN REPORT OF DR. SCHOLZ AT THE NUREMBERG TRIALS, CONCERNING PROPERTY STOLEN FROM FRANCE, MUCH OF WHICH WAS TAKEN TO NEUSCHWANSTEIN

Monuments Men and other workers used a system of pulleys and wooden skids to lower crates of artworks down the steps of the castle.

American GIs hand-carried paintings down the steps of the castle under the supervision of Capt. James Rorimer. In the photograph below, MFAA officer Capt. Edith Standen watches workers carry crates down another set of stairs.

Buxheim

Not far from Neuschwanstein, Monuments Men discovered the studio of Karl Haberstock, the prominent Berlin art dealer and Nazi party member. Haberstock was among the first who suggested to Hitler and Goebbels the possibility of selling "degenerate art" pieces at public auction. In the photograph above, sitting on the easel in the center of the picture, is a painting by the great Spanish artist, Bartolomé Esteban Murillo.
May 1945

Bartolomé Esteban Murillo, *Saint Justa*, c. 1665.
Oil on canvas,
93.4 × 66.4 cm
(36 ¾ × 26 ⅛ in). Meadows Museum, Southern Methodist University, Dallas, Algur H. Meadows Collection, 72.04.

Hamburg

Bells stolen from churches throughout Europe are piled
up in the dock area of Hamburg. There were
approximately 5,000 bells in four groups, many of
which were damaged due to inadequate packing.
August 1945

Race Institute Building

In a corner of the basement were hundreds of Torah scrolls piled 10 feet high. The Race Institute was used by Alfred Rosenberg to research the characteristics of various people overrun by the German Army and under subsequent Nazi rule. American Chaplain Samuel Blinder examines a *Sefer Torah* as he begins the overwhelming task of sorting and inspecting.

July 1945

Unterstein

Soldiers from the 101st Airborne Division—known as the "Screaming Eagles"—requisitioned a local hotel and assembled pieces from Göring's collection to create an impromptu exhibition for journalists and soldiers. This was but a part of Göring's collection, found in a house in Berchtesgaden.

June 1945

Berchtesgaden
Among the looted objects recovered by the 101st
Airborne division were three paintings by Rembrandt,
three paintings by Cranach and a 15th-century
statue of Eve.
June 1945

GIs from the 101st Airborne Division found a cache of sculpture and paintings at one of the bunkers used by Göring to store artwork. In April 1945, Göring frantically ordered the shipment of his most precious works from his palatial estate at Carinhall to Berchtesgaden in southeast Germany. Göring then ordered the destruction of Carinhall to keep it from falling into Russian hands. In the photograph on the right Lt. Gen. Omar Bradley, C.G., 12th U.S. Army Group, enjoys a laugh with officers of the 101st Airborne Division.
May 1945

Two American soldiers unload a wooden statue of the *Madonna with Child* from a freight car abandoned at Berchtesgaden. In the foreground is another sculpture awaiting removal; behind it are more paintings.

Zell-am-see, Austria

Capt. Halsey Hay, of Ft. Edward, New York, and Capt. Harry Anderson,
101st Airborne Division, of Ossining, New York, inspect a painting of
Christ with the Woman Taken in Adultery, which they found in a private home.
This was one of Göring's favorite artworks, which he believed to be by
Jan Vermeer. It later proved to be a forgery.
June 1945

Wewelsburg
Heinrich Himmler's castle at Wewelsburg was a central training ground for racist Nazi ideology. After liberation, inmates of the nearby concentration camp found these stolen paintings inside the castle.

Aalen
Capt. Fred Levy, from Dallas, Texas, opens prize packages from the art collection of Joseph Goebbels. He is holding Albert Cuyp's *Moon Landscape*. On the table is *Rembrandt's Mother*, a painting by Gerrit Dou.
June 1945

Alt Aussee

In many of the mine chambers, Nazi officials had ordered the construction of storage bins to house thousands of paintings and other works of art. The temperature inside the mine varied only 8 degrees (from 40°F in winter to 48°F in summer; 4°C to 9°C) with a fairly constant humidity level of 65%, thus providing tolerable storage conditions.

May 1945

Disaster Averted

Unidentified Monuments officers and mine workers are sitting on five-hundred-pound bombs that had been hidden in crates marked "Marble—Don't Drop" (*Marmor—Nicht Stürzen*). Although Hitler ordered the mine to be sealed to protect the artworks, the district commander—named Eigruber—was intent on destroying its contents. Ironically, Chief of SS Intelligence Kaltenbrunner proved the lesser fanatic and had the bombs removed just days before the arrival of Allied Forces.

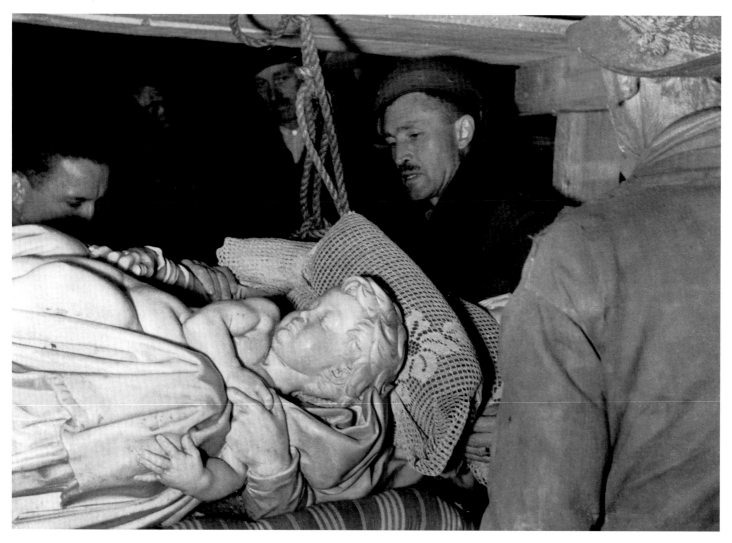

In the photograph above, Monuments officer Lt. Cdr. George Stout struggles to remove the *Bruges Madonna* from the mine. Once outside, it awaits transport to the Munich Collecting Point. Monuments officer Lt. Cdr. Howe later wrote: "The light of our lamps played over the soft folds of the Madonna's robe, the delicate modeling of her face. Her grave eyes looked down, seemed only half aware of the sturdy Child nestling close against her, one hand firmly held in hers."

**Michelangelo, *Bruges
Madonna,* 1503-04.**
Marble, H. 121.9 cm (48 in).
Notre Dame Cathedral,
Bruges, Belgium.

In the photograph above, two unidentified soldiers and Max Eder, an Austrian mine engineer, marvel at several of the *Ghent Altarpiece* panels. In the photograph on the right Lt. Cdr. Stout and others prepare to crate the central panel of the altarpiece.

OPPOSITE

An American GI guards the passage way into the mine chamber containing the *Ghent Altarpiece*. The crate lid is stamped "St. Baafs," in reference to St. Bavo's Cathedral, home of the altarpiece.

**Jan van Eyck, *Ghent
Altarpiece* (interior), 1432.**
Oil on panel,
3.5 × 4.6 m (11 ft 6 in × 15 ft 1 in).
Saint Bavo Cathedral,
Ghent, Belgium.

Van Eyck 1432

Edouard de Rothschild Collection, Paris
This photograph shows a wall in the Rothschild home filled with extraordinary works of art, none more so than Jan Vermeer's *The Astronomer*. Above, left to right: *Surprise Entrance*, Gabriel Metsu; *Woman with Cat*, Flemish School; *Interior*, Pieter de Hooch. Below, left to right: *Young Woman Drinking*, Gerard Terborch; *The Violinist*, Gerrit Dou; *The Astronomer*, Jan Vermeer; *Woman with a Peach*, Frans von Mieiris; *Virgin and Child*, Hans Memling.
Before 1940

Two unidentified soldiers hold Vermeer's *The Astronomer*. This painting was Hitler's most coveted work of art in France. It was among hundreds of artworks stolen from the collection of Edouard de Rothschild in Paris.

OPPOSITE

Jan Vermeer, *The Astronomer*, 1668.
Oil on canvas, 51 × 45 cm (20 × 17 ¾ in).
Louvre, Paris.

Lt. Daniel Kern inspects Jan Vermeer's *The Artist's Studio*. To his right is Max Eder.

Max Eder and an American officer hold Jan Vermeer's *The Artist's Studio* while it is photographed. The painting on the right is by Willem Drost entitled *Portrait of an Officer in a Red Beret*.

OPPOSITE

Jan Vermeer, *The Artist's Studio*, 1665-66.
Oil on canvas, 120 × 100 cm (47 ¼ × 39 ⅜ in).
Kunsthistorisches Museum, Vienna.

COLLECTING POINTS

CHAPTER 7

"It was sort of like running a movie backwards; all the trainloads that had gone to Germany and to the mines and whatever now started coming back. Truckload after truckload and plane loads went back to Belgium, France, Italy.... Once the works got there, committees in those countries were organized to decide who they belonged to and who should get them back, which became a very controversial issue."

LYNN NICHOLAS
AUTHOR, *THE RAPE OF EUROPA*

Challenges facing MFAA officers increased in difficulty and complexity with each discovery of a repository filled with artworks. Security issues, storage conditions, and the pending division of Germany into zones of occupation necessitated the removal of the art to central locations in the American and British Occupation Zones. Finding such large facilities in usable condition in a war-ravaged country was difficult. Although a Collecting Point had been established in Marburg, it quickly became evident that it was too small to store the seemingly endless supply of art being found by Monuments Men and Allied Forces. Further, its northern location was too great a distance from the major repositories being discovered in Bavaria and northern Austria.

On his first trip to Munich, Capt. James Rorimer identified a pair of largely undamaged buildings he considered ideal for the project, known as the Führerbau and the Verwaltungsbau. The buildings had formerly housed Hitler's office and the Nazi Party headquarters. There were competing interests for the use of these buildings: General Patton wanted to establish his regional headquarters in Hitler's former office—another example of the billeting issues MFAA officers regularly confronted. In this instance, General Patton yielded. The task of setting up a suitable facility was assigned to Lt. Craig Hugh Smyth, a naval officer who had, prior to his military service, been one of the first curators at the National Gallery in Washington. Lt. Smyth had

Munich Collecting Point
A U.S. Army truck backed up to the Collecting Point, where workers unloaded its contents.
Summer 1945

also overseen the packing and shipping of the National Gallery's most important paintings to the Biltmore Estate, in January, 1942.

The Munich Collecting Point became the prototype for others that followed. Two other facilities were set up in Wiesbaden and Offenbach. In each location similar procedures were followed. The buildings were secured, cleaned, and staffed. Basic equipment such as desks, typewriters, and material to set up carpentry shops, was obtained. The ongoing problem of wartime shortages made even the simple tasks difficult. Entire art reference libraries had to be assembled to enable documentation of all incoming items. Receiving areas were created, but because shipments began arriving before storage bins and shelving could be constructed, the art was initially stacked on the floor.

When a shipment arrived, each item was logged in, then evaluated to determine exactly what it was and, when possible, its country of origin. In many instances, such as that of the French Rothschild family's numerous belongings found at Neuschwanstein, the artwork was so famous that identification of the piece and its origin was simple. Because most of these stolen works had not been removed from their original shipping crates, Monuments Men put them on a train and sent them directly back to Paris for French authorities to further process. The same procedure was followed with the Veit Stoss altarpiece in Nuremberg. Because MFAA officers knew it had been stolen by the Nazis from the Church of Our Lady in Cracow, they crated and returned it directly to Cracow using German General von Ribbentrop's personal railway car.

Until identification and sorting could be completed, MFAA officers were responsible for the protection and stewardship of some of the world's greatest art treasures.

Using their considerable expertise, they set up Collecting Points to function like the museums which had been the training ground for so many of the Monuments officers. Photography studios were created which enabled staff to forward photographs of stolen works to art experts in other countries for additional information. Conservation labs were established to facilitate the restoration of books, paintings, and other objects that had suffered from harsh treatment during their odyssey.

The Munich Collecting Point primarily housed art stolen by the ERR, Hitler and Göring's purchases and thefts, and the contents of repositories found in Western occupied areas such as Alt Aussee. The Wiesbaden Collecting Point, set up by Capt. Walter Farmer, housed art from Berlin's vast and rich museums discovered at the mine in Merkers. It also contained art from other German museums found in Siegen, Grasleben, and other mines where items had been placed for safekeeping by museum officials. The third major Collecting Point was established in an unbombed I.G. Farben building in Offenbach near Frankfurt. The obstacles MFAA officers faced at Offenbach were formidable. The Offenbach Collecting Point contained ERR loot from Masonic Lodges and Jewish libraries and synagogues. The condition of many of these items was dreadful. Many of the millions of books waiting to be sorted had detached pages that required individual analysis. Ancient Torah Scrolls and other such artifacts, all of which required detailed and painstaking review, lay in piles.

In time, the chaotic environment that plagued the initial weeks of the Collecting Points gave way to a well-organized operation. Monuments Men began rebuilding a cultural atmosphere in Germany, void of Nazi propaganda, by using the artworks in their custody to create exhibitions attended by GIs and civilians alike. In many ways their actions jump-started cultural life in Germany after the war.

Munich

A view across Königsplatz with the Munich Collecting Point clearly visible in the distance (just to the right of the street lamp at left). In the distance and to the left of this lamp are the two Helden Temples, since destroyed. Much of the enormous paved area of Königsplatz has been replaced with grass. The Munich Collecting Point was secured with barbed wire until more permanent measures could be implemented. Note the American flag hanging from the balcony and the Nazi eagle above the terrace (left of the flag), subsequently removed by GIs.
June 1945

The photograph above shows the condition of one of the building's rooms when MFAA officials arrived. After only a few weeks of intense preparation, this space became the Office of the Registrar.

MFAA officials had to build art reference libraries to aid in the identification of works of art, and to enable them to trace their ownership prior to commencing the restitution process. As time passed, the organization of the Collecting Point greatly improved. Badly needed resources—things as simple as easels on which paintings could be placed for analysis—were obtained or constructed.

The pace of deliveries of artworks from the various repositories initially exceeded the readiness of Collecting Point officials to receive them. Temporary storage rooms were created for paintings, sculpture and other works until storage bins, such as those in the photograph above, could be constructed.

The supply of art arriving at the Collecting Point seemed endless. The sorting
of it was exhausting work.

By the time of this photograph, the system for evaluating stolen works of art had become refined and more efficient. A library containing critically important art reference books had been assembled, a portion of which are visible in the background. A card catalogue system was created to maintain an inventory of works. Larger paintings were placed on easels to facilitate analysis. Each of the three paintings on view is a masterpiece. Those on each end were part of the loot stolen by the Hermann Göring Division from the Monte Cassino repository during the time they were purportedly "safeguarding" it. The table in the foreground was formerly in Hitler's office.

Titian (Tiziano Vecellio),
***Danaë*, c. 1550-60.**
Oil on canvas,
117 × 69 cm (46 × 27 ⅛ in).
Museo Nazionale di Capodimonte,
Naples.

**Bartolomé Esteban
Murillo, *Saint Rufina*,
c. 1665.**
Oil on canvas,
93.4 × 66.4 cm (36 × 28 in).
Meadows Museum,
Southern Methodist
University, Dallas, Algur H.
Meadows Collection,
72.05.

**Pieter Brueghel the Elder, *The
Blind Leading the Blind*, 1568.**
Tempera on canvas, 86 × 154 cm
(33 ⅞ × 60 ⅝ in). Museo Nazionale
di Capodimonte, Naples.

Collecting Point staff had a variety of tasks to perform.
One important step was photographing each work of art.

MFAA officials were not passive caretakers of the extraordinary masterpieces that arrived at the Collecting Point. Careful evaluation of the condition of key works identified those in need of conservation. In this photograph, a restorer works on a painting by Bernardo Bellotto that once hung in the destroyed Royal Castle in Warsaw. In the background on the left is Leonardo da Vinci's *Lady With an Ermine*.

Standing with three famous paintings by Raphael from the Alte Pinakothek in Munich are, from left to right: Daniel Knight of Powersville, Missouri; Samuel R. Rosenbaum of Patterson, New Jersey; and Frederick R. Pleasants of Upper Montelair, New Jersey. All of these men were War Department civilians for OMGB, and members of the Collecting Point staff.
November 1946

Raphael, *Tempi Madonna*, c. 1507.
Oil on panel, 75 × 51 cm (29 ½ × 20 in).
Alte Pinakothek, Munich.

Raphael, *The Canigiani Holy Family*, c. 1507.
Oil on panel, 131 × 107 cm (51 ½ × 42 ⅛ in).
Alte Pinakothek, Munich.

Raphael, *Madonna della Tenda* (*Madonna of the Curtain*), c. 1513-14.
Oil on panel, 65.8 × 51.2 cm (25 ⅞ × 20 ⅛ in).
Alte Pinakothek, Munich.

Wiesbaden Collecting Point
Sgt. Kenneth C. Lindsay and others admire the *Portrait of a Young Man*, attributed to the Studio of Botticelli.

In the photograph above, Capt. Edith Standen (left) and Rose Valland (right) are holding paintings while posing next to a medieval suit of armor awaiting restitution. In the upper right photograph, a recently-arrived sculpture by the great French artist, Aristide Maillol, has been tagged "Wiesbaden no. 31." In the photograph on the right, Capt. Standen walks past workers as another shipment of art is unloaded.
May 1946

Offenbach Collecting Point
Maurice Liber, Director of the Rabbinic School of France,
helps identify Jewish books and manuscripts.

*"...in the sorting room I would come to a box of books which the sorters
had brought together into one fold...books from a library which once had
been in some distant town in Poland, or an extinct Yeshiva. There was
something sad and mournful about these volumes...as if they were whispering a tale of yearning and hope long since obliterated.*

*I would pick up a badly worn Talmud with hundreds of names of
many generations of students and scholars. What were they now? Or,
rather where were their ashes?.... I would find myself straightening
out these books and arranging them in the boxes with a personal sense
of tenderness.... How difficult it is to look at the contents of the
depot with the detachment of someone evaluating property or with the
impersonal viewpoint of scholarly evaluation."*

U.S. ARMY CAPT. ISAAC BENCOWITZ, MONUMENTS, FINE ARTS, AND ARCHIVES OFFICER

OPPOSITE

More than 600 Torah scrolls
were found in the American
sector of Germany. While
stacked like kindling, the Allies
took care to tightly bind the
scrolls to keep them intact and
protect the sacred text within.
Compare this to the haphazard
and damaging handling of scrolls
in the Race Institute Building.
SEE PAGES 184-185.

Books and other archival material were stored until they could be evaluated and sorted. Millions of books were stolen by the Nazis from more than sixty libraries throughout Europe and Russia. In the general sorting room (center), libraries of the Western countries were separated from those of Eastern countries, each of which were assigned a different floor of the building. Another floor was used to store books whose origins could not easily be identified. Sorters handled, on average, 30,000 books per day. In the photograph at left, wet books and manuscripts were treated in the Care and Preservation Room prior to sorting and restitution. Note the clothesline where damaged pages were hung to dry.

U.S. Army Capt. Isaac Bencowitz (center) poses with Major N. Hocoraebbu and Major V.M. Ivanoff, both Russian officers. Behind them are crates of books that were stolen by German troops and later recovered by Allied Forces. The books in these crates have been sorted and grouped by Russian cities of origin for restitution. Officials at the Collecting Point regularly liaised with representatives from various countries in Europe to coordinate the return of stolen works.

HOMEWARD BOUND

CHAPTER 8

"...no historical grievance will rankle so long, or be the cause of so much justified bitterness, as the removal, for any reason, of a part of the heritage of any nation, even if that heritage may be interpreted as a prize of war. And though this removal may be done with every intention of altruism, we are none the less convinced that it is our duty, individually and collectively, to protest against it, and that though our obligations are to the nation to which we owe allegiance, there are yet further obligation to common justice, decency, and the establishment of the power of right, not of expediency or might, among civilized nations."

"WIESBADEN MANIFESTO," AN INTERNAL LETTER OF PROTEST SIGNED BY 24 MFAA OFFICERS CONCERNING REMOVAL OF GERMAN-OWNED ART WORKS TO THE UNITED STATES NOVEMBER 7, 1945

"Stalin rose and gripped the back of his chair with such force that his brown hands went white at the knuckles. He spat out his words as if they burnt his mouth. Great stretches of his country had been laid to waste, he said, and the peasants put to the sword. Reparations should be paid to the countries that had suffered most. While he was speaking, nobody moved."

HARRY HOPKINS, PERSONAL REPRESENTATIVE, ADVISOR AND AIDE TO PRESIDENT ROOSEVELT SPEAKING ON DISCUSSIONS HELD AT YALTA, FEBRUARY 4-11, 1945

The first token shipment to Holland of twenty-six paintings, being loaded aboard a U.S. Army airplane at Munich, with pilots and Lt. Colonel Vorenkamp, Lt. Smyth and an unidentified Dutch representative present.

Establishing the Collecting Points and getting them operational was a monumental accomplishment further complicated by the eagerness of foreign government officials to retrieve works of art stolen by the Nazis. Officials in Washington, mindful of maintaining good relations with the allies, were equally anxious to extricate the United States Army from such a complicated situation. As an interim measure, and on the recommendation of MFAA officer John Nicholas Brown, General Eisenhower ordered the immediate return of universally recognized works of art, in bulk where possible, on a rotation basis while the process of sorting and identifying other works at the Collecting Points continued.

The first shipment from Neuschwanstein Castle to French officials in Paris required the use of twenty-two railcars containing 634 cases of art, furniture, and other precious objects. A second trainload of thirteen railcars departed a month later followed by the final shipment of four railcars. In all, Monuments Men removed from the Neuschwanstein repository more than 6,000 items packed in 1,200 crates. Also easing the burden on MFAA officials were the discoveries in Campo Tures and San Leonardo, Italy, of art stolen from Florentine museums, principally the Uffizi. Monuments Men arranged for direct shipment of these art treasures to Florence requiring the use of thirteen railcars. Upon arrival at the Florence rail yards the contents were loaded onto United States Army trucks and delivered to the Piazza Signoria by Monuments Men—including Capt. Deane Keller and Lt. Frederick Hartt. The troops and their shipment received a heroes' welcome from the mayor, other officials, and a delirious citizenry. With these returns the work of MFAA officials in Italy was largely finished.

During the next twelve months MFAA officers at each of the three Collecting Points organized and, in most instances, accompanied the most famous works back "home." First to be returned was the *Ghent Altarpiece* in August, 1945, which was loaded into ten crates and shipped by air to Belgium. The *Bruges Madonna* followed in September, still wrapped in the blankets in which she had been removed from the salt mine at Alt Aussee by MFAA Lt. Cdr. Stout. Fifty of the finest paintings stolen from France were shipped to Paris. MFAA officer James Rorimer arranged for seventy-three cases containing the stained glass from Strasbourg to be returned directly to the Cathedral from the Heilbronn mine. In October, 1945, a shipment of major works stolen from Dutch museums, including paintings by Rubens and Rembrandt, and Göring's beloved painting by Vermeer (later determined to be a fake), was returned to Holland. MFAA advisor Andrew Ritchie hand delivered Vermeer's *The Artist's Studio* to Austria, and a multitude of other important works followed.

The Veit Stoss altarpiece was a particularly challenging problem due both to its size and the devastation of Nuremberg, where it had been found. In all, twenty-seven railcars were needed for its return to Poland along with two of three Czartoryski paintings: Rembrandt's *Landscape with Parable of the Good Samaritan* and Leonardo da Vinci's *Lady With an Ermine*. Accompanying this shipment was Major Karol Estreicher, senior officer from Poland assigned to the Munich Collecting Point. Estreicher, whose brother had died in Nazi captivity, hung Polish and American flags on the side of the railcars as they arrived in Cracow in early May, 1946. Because of a tense and increasingly unstable political climate, MFAA officials had to leave Poland suddenly. Years later, while visiting Cracow, Monuments officer John Nicholas Brown and Estreicher went to mass to see the restored Veit Stoss altarpiece at the Church of Our Lady. The priest celebrating mass that day became, decades later, His Holiness Pope John Paul II.

By 1947 contents of the large repositories had been removed and logged in at one of the Collecting Points. Monuments officials continued to find missing works, but on a far more limited basis. While pressure from officials in Washington to expedite returns and close the Collecting Points increased, the large number of unclaimed items, in particular those of Jewish origin with no known heirs, were a problem for MFAA officials. To aid in the restitution process, two organizations were formed to represent Jewish groups throughout Europe. These arrangements came to fruition early in 1949. Even then, State Department officials were unable to close the Collecting Points until September, 1951, and only then with the assistance of two MFAA veterans: Lt. Cdr. Thomas Howe and Lt. Cdr. Lane Faison. Responsibility for the unclaimed items that remained passed to a German agency, which for the next ten years acted as a trustee to oversee additional returns. The epic saga, however, did not end there.

In the years 1945-1951, millions of items were received at the Collecting Points, most of which were subsequently returned to the countries of origin, even in some instances, the place from which they had been stolen. Records indicate that hundreds of thousands of artworks and other belongings were logged into Munich, Wiesbaden, and Offenbach Collecting Points. However, entries for complete collections were often treated as a single item, e.g., entire libraries containing as many as a million books. That MFAA officials could almost overnight create and make operational the Collecting Point facilities in war-ravaged Germany, identify ownership of millions of items, then arrange for their safe return, is a testament to the character and sense of duty of these remarkable men and women.

Russia

A very different approach to restitutions was taken by the Soviets. The devastating loss of life and scorched-earth policy of Hitler and the Nazis resulted in so great a hatred that art found in sectors controlled by the Soviet Union was returned to a new home—Russia.

At the historic Yalta Conference in February, 1945, Roosevelt, Churchill, and Stalin addressed the dismemberment of Germany and issued a protocol concerning reparations to be extricated from Germany:

"…the Moscow reparation commission should take in its initial studies as a basis for discussion the suggestion of the Soviet Government that the total sum of the reparation…should be $22 billion dollars [equivalent to $245 billion in 2005] and that 50 per cent should go to the Union of Soviet Socialist Republics."

Payment would be made "in kind" by removals, and to a lesser extent the future use of German labor and delivery of goods. Removals were to be made within two years of war's end and would include "equipment, machine tools, ships, rolling stock, German investments abroad, shares of industrial, transport and other enterprises in Germany, etc., these removals to be carried out chiefly for the purpose of destroying the war potential of Germany." Although the protocol stated that the $22 billion sum was only "a basis for discussion," Stalin later claimed that Roosevelt and Churchill had agreed to the amount.

Russian officials created uniformed brigades of art historians and other art professionals. Together with Red Army soldiers these so-called "trophy brigades" located and recovered works of art including that stolen from Russian museums and palaces. Eventually, anything of value was taken home for use in Russia's reconstruction. Most cultural items were deposited at the Hermitage Museum in Leningrad and the Pushkin Museum in Moscow. At the time, these activities were seen by many as fully justified reparations consistent with the Yalta protocol. And with the emergence of the Cold War so soon after the end of World War II, the attention of the United States focused on much larger geopolitical issues. Europeans were busy simply trying to feed their people and rebuild their shattered countries.

In the 1950s many if not most of the artworks removed by Soviet forces from Germany and Poland were returned to the museums of origin in Soviet bloc countries in a gesture of goodwill. But other works, in particular paintings formerly owned by private German collectors, were secretly placed in storage at various Soviet museums, where they sat quietly for forty-five years.

With the fall of Communism, a new Russia gradually emerged. The secrecy that had been such a defining characteristic of communist rule gave way to a more open environment. It was an awkward process involving accusations and conflict. The public affirmation in 1991 of so-called "trophy art" by Nikolai Gubenko, the last Minister of Culture of the Soviet era, created a controversy which festers today as Germany, Poland, and others seek the return of items once in their possession. It has become an emotional debate and has, as a consequence, become a path to visibility for some politicians. After years of being sequestered, these magnificent paintings, in a superlative state of preservation, now hang openly in the Hermitage and Pushkin Museums. Some lesser-quality works hang in study galleries available to art historians.

The Hague Convention of 1907 prohibited the looting of cultural treasures and private property. It allowed for no exceptions. However, events in the Soviet Union from 1941-1944 were, by any historical standard, exceptional. Consider their perspective: more than 25 million people killed of whom 16 million were civilians; 82,000 elementary and secondary schools and 334 colleges damaged or destroyed; 6,000 hospitals destroyed or plundered; 427 out of the 992 museums in the Soviet Union destroyed; almost 2,500 churches and 532 synagogues partially damaged or destroyed. Virtually everything of value was stolen. Further, German leaders made every effort to destroy all symbols of Russian culture and achievement, including the homes and work places of Leo Tolstoy, Peter Tchaikovsky, Pushkin, Chekhov, and countless others.

At the Piskariovskoye Cemetery, located on the outskirts of present day St. Petersburg, there is a memorial honoring the almost one million victims of the 900-day blockade of the city. On its wall is the following inscription:

Here lie Leningraders, Here lie citizens—men, women and children. Beside them lie Red Army soldiers. They defended you with their lives, Leningrad, the cradle of the Revolution. We would not be able to give their noble names here for so many of them lie under the everlasting guard of granite. Looking at these stones, remember: no one has been forgotten and nothing has been forgotten.

The enemy, clad in armour and iron, was forcing its way into the city. But workers, schoolchildren, teachers, civil guards stood up together with the army, and said, all as one: sooner death will be scared by us than we will be scared by death. We have not forgotten the famine-stricken, ferocious, dark winter of forty-one—forty-two, nor the fierce bombardments and savage bombings of forty-three. The entire city land had been pierced. None of your lives, comrades, have been forgotten. Under continuous fire from the sky, land and water you performed your everyday feat simply and with dignity. And together with the fatherland you all have gained the victory. So let the grateful people, the Motherland and the hero-city of Leningrad forever bow down their banners to your immortal lives in this field of solemn sorrow.

Sixty years have passed since the end of the "Great Patriotic War" as it is still known in Russia, but people's memories of these horrific events and their sense of loss are ever present. Only in this full context is it possible for those of us who are not Russian to understand their deeply rooted feelings on this subject.

ITALY

Campo Tures

Capt. Deane Keller and Professor Filippo Rossi, Director of Galleries, Florence, stand in front of two crates containing Michelangelo's *Bacchus* (left) and Donatello's *St. George* (right). These and hundreds of other priceless artworks were stolen by German troops from repositories that contained masterworks from other Florentine museums. In the photograph below, workers use a special truck-mounted crane to aid in the removal of the crates for their trip home.

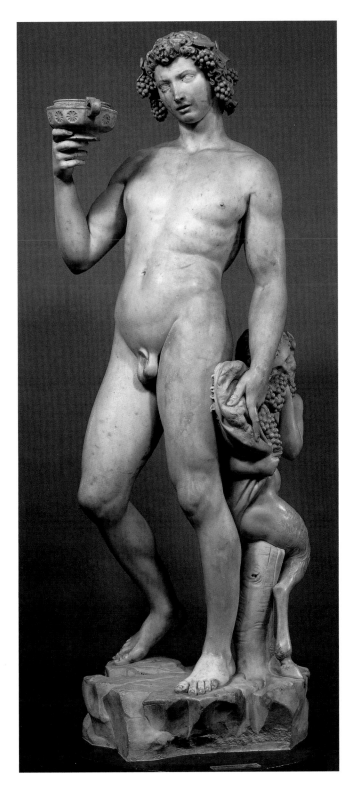

Michelangelo, *Bacchus*, 1497.
Marble, H. 2 m (6 ft 8 in).
Museo Nazionale del Bargello, Florence.

Donatello, *St. George*, c. 1415-17.
Marble, H. 1.96 m (6 ft 5 in).
Museo Nazionale del Bargello, Florence.

San Leonardo

In their hasty retreat towards German-controlled Austria, German soldiers had a difficult time finding enough space to store all the stolen paintings in their possession. They settled on the use of an abandoned jail which, although too small to hold all the paintings, was adequate to house some of them. These two important paintings by Bellini and Lippi were found, with virtually no protective wrapping, on the floor of the jail.

Giovanni Bellini, *Pietá*, c. 1495.
Tempera on panel, 76 × 121 cm
(29 ⅞ × 47 ⅔ in). Uffizi, Florence.

Filippo Lippi,
Adoration of the
***Child*, c. 1483.**
Oil on panel,
96 × 71 cm
(37 ¾ × 27 ⅞ in).
Uffizi, Florence.

Homecoming
The recovered stolen works from the Florence museums were shipped by train from northern Italy, and then loaded onto U.S. Army trucks that transported them to jubilant crowds and officials in the Piazza Signoria.
July 1945

Capt. Deane Keller, second from the right, supervised the loading of priceless artworks onto trucks for their delivery to the museums in Florence. The man on the left is Professor Filippo Rossi.

The Florence Guard of Honor plays a fanfare as U.S. 1st Army trucks return part of Florence's priceless art treasures to Italian officials and other dignitaries in the Piazza Signoria. Professor Gaetano Pieraccini, Mayor of Florence, delivered his remarks after the paintings were returned to the city of Florence. Seated behind the dais is Maj. Gen. Edgar Hume, Senior Civil Affairs Officer, U.S. 5th Army, and on his right Brig. Gen. F.J. Tate, CG.

Florence

Dr. Cesare Fasola and others eagerly examine one of the early returns of art from its hiding place at Montegufoni. He later commented, "All works of art for whose fate we still tremble will return to us, bringing the light of their beauty to attract, as before, pilgrims from every country and to inspire thoughts of peace."

Venice

The *Winged Lion of St. Mark* had been removed for safekeeping from its perch high atop the column bounded by the Doges Palace, Piazza San Marco, and the canals. In these photographs workers tow the Lion into position through the Palazzo Ducale courtyard before hoisting it back to its original position where it once again greets all visitors.

May 1945

FRANCE

OPPOSITE

Mona Lisa Returns

Monuments officer Capt. Rorimer and an unidentified Louvre official stand before the empty space where the *Mona Lisa* was displayed before the onset of the war. Written on the wall is "La Joconde," as she is known in France. The other photographs document the dramatic return and unveiling of the painting in the Louvre after almost six years in hiding.

Leonardo da Vinci, *Mona Lisa*, 1503.
Oil on panel,
77 × 53 cm
(30 ⅓ × 20 ⅞ in).
Louvre, Paris.

In keeping with orders from Gen. Eisenhower to make immediate restitutions of key works to Allied countries, MFAA officials organized the first of many convoys. This one headed for France with 71 stolen paintings found at repositories in Germany. The convoy is driving through Königsplatz having just departed the Munich Collecting Point.
November 1945

Maj. Edward E. Adams, Q.M.C., the officer who oversaw the removal and shipment of artworks from Neuschwanstein back to Paris, wrote the following: "The large painting was the *Three Graces*, painted by Rubens. It was too large to fit in the standard closed freight car, so we made a special tight plywood box, lined with waterproof paper, insulated it against frost with excelsior padding, and shipped it on a flat-car. When completed, the crate measured 2.75 meters squared by 30 centimeters thick [9 feet × 1 foot]. A scaffold of heavy planks was constructed on the flatcar and the crate was set upright on edge and lashed securely to this framework. Even then we had to slope the scaffold thirty degrees in order to clear tunnels. After the crate was in place it was covered by two heavy tarpaulins."

The *Burghers of Calais*, by
Auguste Rodin, sits on the
back of a truck at the Munich
Collecting Point.

Auguste Rodin,
***Burghers of Calais*, 1884-86.**
Bronze. Rodin Museum, Paris.

HOLLAND

Stolen Streetcars

Loaded on to flatbed railcars in the Bremen Yards are some of the 300 streetcars stolen from Amsterdam by the Nazis. The streetcars are in the process of being shipped back to Holland. Two Dutch teams worked in concert with U.S. Military government officials for more than eight months to identify property stolen from Holland. A considerable amount of items ranging from streetcars to table linens, were located in the Bremen enclave.

June 1946

BELGIUM

The *Bruges Madonna* has been loaded aboard a truck at the Munich Collecting Point for its return to Belgium in the same wrappings used by Lt. Cdr. George L. Stout when it was removed from the salt mine at Alt Aussee.
September 1945

A case containing a panel of the *Ghent Altarpiece* is being loaded onto a truck prior to its flight home to Belgium. Supervising from the doorway are Lts. Thomas Howe and Craig Smyth.
August 21, 1945

Brussels
The *Ghent Altarpiece* was put on display in Brussels before its final return home.

DENMARK

The *Lion of Isted* is a monument commemorating the Danish-Prussian war of 1848-1850. German soldiers stole the statue from the Flensburg cemetery in Denmark and installed it at the Adolf Hitler Barracks, a cadet school in Berlin. U.S. Army Engineers faced a considerable challenge figuring out the best way to remove the statue and prepare it for transport. U.S. Army Col. Barney Oldfield (right) assisted with its return to Denmark, where it may now be seen at the Tøjhusmuseum in Copenhagen.

March 1946

AUSTRIA

Hofburg Palace, Vienna
Sgt. Jack N. Corbett of Oakland, California, a former art student at the University of California, views Raphael's *Madonna of the Meadows* from the Kunsthistorisches Museum in Vienna. In the lower left photograph, Mr. Peer Oppenheimer of PRO, USACA looks at a late *Self Portrait* by Rubens.
February 1946

Monuments Men examine Holy Roman Regalia upon its return to Vienna. From left to right are an unidentified officer, Civilian Advisor Dr. Andrew Ritchie, Lt. Perry Cott, and Lt. Ernest DeWald.

This portrait of *Philip IV, King of Spain,* by the great Spanish artist Diego Velázquez, is admired by Gen. Mark W. Clark, CG, USFA, the host of a ceremony to celebrate the return of art treasures recovered by the U.S. Army. The general's guests are Lt. Gen. Emile Marie Berthourart of France, Lt. Gen. R.L. McCreery of Britain, Mr. Figil, Chancellor of Austria, and Col. Gen. Alexis Zheltov, Russian Deputy Commander.
December 1946

POLAND

German workmen and American GIs got their last look at the head of one of the main figures from the Veit Stoss altarpiece as it was being packed in Nuremberg for its return home to Cracow.
April 1945

Veit Stoss, *Saint Mary Altarpiece (Veit Stoss Altarpiece)*, 1477-89.
Wood, polychrome,
H. 14m (46 ft).
Cathedral of Our Lady, Cracow.

Returning Da Vinci

Major Karol Estreicher, Polish Liaison Officer, signed a release to take into custody the Polish-owned works of art for their return home. Major Estreicher draped the Polish and American flags from the train as it approached the station in Cracow. With the train as a backdrop, Major Estreicher, MFAA officer Lt. Frank P. Albright of Baltimore, MD, and two unidentified American GIs providing security stopped to enjoy a last look at one of Leonardo da Vinci's masterworks before its return to Cracow.
April 1946

OPPOSITE

Leonardo da Vinci, *Lady With an Ermine (Portrait of Cecilia Gallerani)*, c. 1483-88.
Oil on panel, 55 × 40 cm
(21 ⅔ × 15 ¾ in).
Czartoryski Museum, Cracow.

RUSSIA'S PROLONGED TRAGEDY

Starvation

Almost one million people died during the 900-day siege of Leningrad, many from starvation. Winters were harsh and the ground frozen making burials virturally impossible until late spring. Mustering the energy on a starvation diet for such a gruesome task was, ironically, a death-defying effort. During most of the 900-day siege the city was cut off from food shipments. Parks and other open areas were used as agriculture fields to grow anything possible to keep people alive. In the photograph above, a small cabbage field has been planted in front of St. Isaac's Cathedral. The photograph on the left came from a Russian archive. A Russian wrote the following caption: "In September [1941], pets were still a customary attribute of the prewar life. In October, their number noticeably reduced and by winter, they totally disappeared."

Cultural Obliteration

German soldiers desecrated the Tchaikovsky Museum and used it for a motorcycle repair garage.

"We are barbarians and we wish to be barbarians.
It is an honorable calling."

ADOLF HITLER

Abandoned Loot

Red Army soldiers sort through paintings, some still crated, that were looted and later abandoned by German soldiers as they fled Eastern Prussia. These artworks were among pieces stolen from Catherine Palace and Peterhof.

Pushkin Museum

Soviet officials unload trucks containing thousands of artworks removed from Germany. In the photograph above, the young woman in the lower left corner is Irina Antonova, who would later become the Director of the Pushkin Museum in Moscow.

In the name of the people of the United States of America, I present this scroll to the City of Leningrad as a memorial to its gallant soldiers and to its loyal men, women and children who, isolated from the rest of their nation by the invader and despite constant bombardment and untold sufferings from cold, hunger and sickness, successfully defended their beloved city throughout the critical period September 8, 1941 to January 18, 1943, and thus symbolized the undaunted spirit of the peoples of the Union of Soviet Socialist Republics and of all the nations of the world resisting forces of aggression.

May 17 1944

Franklin D. Roosevelt

Washington, D. C.

Recognition

In a cover letter to Joseph Stalin which accompanied the scroll reproduced on this page, President Roosevelt wrote the following:

"My dear Marshal Stalin:
I am sending to you two scrolls for Stalingrad and Leningrad, which cities have won the wholehearted admiration of the American people. The heroism of the citizens of these two cities and the soldiers who so ably defended them has not only been an inspiration to the people of the United States, but has served to bind even more closely the friendship of our two nations. Stalingrad and Leningrad have become synonyms for the fortitude and endurance which has enabled us to resist and will finally enable us to overcome the aggression of our enemies.
I hope that in presenting these scrolls to the two cities you will see fit to convey to their citizens my own personal expressions of friendship and admiration and my hope that our people will continue to develop that close understanding which has marked our common effort.
Very sincerely yours,
Franklin D. Roosevelt"

"...SOONER DEATH WILL BE SCARED BY US..."

This excerpt, from the defiant inscription on the wall at Piskariovskoye Memorial Cemetery, symbolizes the extraordinary determination of Leningraders to survive. (See page 229 for the entire inscription). More than half a million people were buried at this cemetery between 1941 and 1944. Corpses were delivered in such quantity that officials could not continue to maintain records of the dead and where they were buried. Burial mounds exist today that were once common pits. Each mound has a single stone grave-marker with the year and either a star if those buried were soldiers, or a hammer and sickle if they were civilians.

A slice of bread, grains of salt, and a candle: basic necessities that determined who lived—and who died—during the Blockade, as it is known in Russia. An elderly gentleman arranged these items atop one of the many mass burial mounds while visiting the cemetery.
St. Petersburg, November 2005

CASUALTIES OF WAR

CHAPTER 9

"Germany will either be a world power or will not exist at all."
ADOLF HITLER

"If the war is to be lost, the nation also will perish. This fate is inevitable. There is no need to consider the basis even of a most primitive existence any longer. On the contrary, it is better to destroy even that, and to destroy ourselves. The nation has proved itself weak, and the future belongs solely to the stronger eastern nation. Besides, those who remain after the battle are of little value; for the good have fallen."
ADOLF HITLER, CONVERSATION WITH ARMAMENTS MINISTER ALBERT SPEER
MARCH 18, 1945

The casualties of World War II were monumental: the death of at least 50 million people, more than half of whom were civilians; architectural triumphs, cultural masterpieces, and personal property destroyed and still missing; a way of life lost. Allied Forces added to the damage in their costly drive to end Nazi tyranny, moving first into Italy, and then France on D-Day. Some looting by Allied troops occurred, most by soldiers wanting souvenirs. In contrast, Hitler's scorched-earth operations in Eastern Europe and Russia and his theft of cultural treasures throughout Europe were deliberate, organized campaigns to destroy people and all evidence of their society.

Italy suffered horrific architectural losses in the course of Allied efforts to dislodge entrenched German troops. Allied bombs which targeted rail centers and industrial facilities, too frequently damaged or destroyed nearby churches. In Padua, the thirteenth century Eremitani Church, containing a series of frescoes by Andrea Mantegna, was reduced to fragments. The Teatro Carlo Felice in Genoa was severely damaged by fire caused by bombing. While the highest profile loss at the hand of the Allies was the destruction of the Abbey of Monte Cassino, the devastation of

A view of the Ponte Vecchio, the only one of Florence's six main bridges not destroyed by the retreating German troops.
August 1944

the extraordinary series of frescoes in the Campo Santo of Pisa was the most significant loss of an artistic treasure. German troops had occupied the Leaning Tower, using its elevation to spot Allied troops, then calling in their coordinates to field artillery headquarters. In the process of returning fire, Allied troops unintentionally hit the Campo Santo causing the roof to catch fire and collapse. The extreme heat of the fire blistered most of the frescoes and destroyed many others. MFAA officer Capt. Keller utilized U.S. Army engineers to construct provisional roofs to protect what remained of the frescoes while arranging for experts from Florence to begin the tedious process of gathering the pieces for future restoration.

In stark contrast, concern for the well-being of Italian cultural treasures was not shared by Hitler and Field Marshal Kesselring, Commander of German Forces in Italy. In an effort to delay the steady advance of Allied Forces, Kesselring ordered the destruction of all bridges in Florence with the exception of the Ponte Vecchio, and even it was mined. Some believe Hitler spared this bridge out of affection. More likely it was because the bridge's narrow passageway provided limited use by vehicular traffic, especially tanks. The demolition charges used by German forces vastly exceeded what was necessary to destroy the bridges causing enormous collateral damage to the adjacent palaces and towers, most of which had been built in the fourteenth century. The bomb blasts blew out the windows of the adjacent Uffizi Gallery. A considerable portion of what had constituted medieval Florence was gone forever. Gone, too, was the Ponte Santa Trinita and its beautiful sculptures of the *Four Seasons*.

Had Hitler's orders in Western Europe been fully implemented, some cities might have resembled those in the East. In Paris, Hitler informed General Dietrich von Choltitz, German commander of the city, that Paris "must be utterly destroyed. On the departure of the Wehrmacht, nothing must be left standing, no church, no artistic monument." Hitler wanted the city's water supply cut off to insure that the "ruined city may be a prey to epidemics." A subsequent order from Hitler instructed Choltitz to destroy all bridges crossing the Seine River. "Paris must not fall into the hands of the enemy except as a field of ruins." In the end, Choltitz's appreciation of the city's beauty and his knowledge that any such acts would serve no military purpose, spared Paris from the fate of Warsaw.

Other cities in France were not as lucky. A large number of towns in the Normandy area were severely damaged by Allied Forces trying to establish a foothold on French soil. In explaining why damage to churches seemed disproportionate to other area structures, MFAA officer Capt. James Rorimer said:

"Before and during battle a historic monument was no more sacred to the Germans than any military installation. Again and again they used church towers as observation posts, and snipers fired from them at our advancing troops."

As the noose tightened around Hitler and the German Army, the stage was set for the final act of a twelve year nightmare. The Führer Bunker was the stage; the "audience" consisted of three million Berliners Hitler refused to evacuate and the invading Soviet Army soldiers arriving by the hundreds of thousands. In the end, Hitler was determined to destroy that which he could no longer control. Hitler was reluctant to accept any responsibility for defeat, saying only that he was excessively tolerant and insufficiently ruthless.

Despite pleas from Berlin museum directors and others, in particular Albert Speer, Hitler refused to allow most of the German museum paintings and other artworks to be evacuated on the grounds that such requests were defeatist. Finally, in March, 1945, less than two months before the fall of Berlin, some of the art was moved to underground mines, Merkers in particular. By that late date, proper packing materials were unavailable. Without notice, paintings arrived at the Kaiserode and Grasleben mines. The last convoy didn't leave Berlin until April 7. In contrast, Göring and other party leaders had long since begun shipping their stolen art and other belongings to the alpine region of Berchtesgaden and other places.

But not everything left Berlin. More than four hundred paintings from the Kaiser-Friedrich and Deutsche Museums, among them masterpieces of the highest order, remained behind in bomb-proof shelters. Other paintings, sculptures, and icons—such as the Pergamon Altar (dating to 180 BCE) and the Gold Treasure of Priam (from the ancient city of Troy), excavated by a German archeologist in 1872—had also been stored by desperate German museum officials. The size of many objects either precluded their transportation to the mine repositories, or they were too large to fit through mine entrances.

Beginning in 1940, officials in Berlin constructed six massive flak-towers (*flaktürme*) as an integral part of the city's defense system, each of which could provide shelter for up to 18,000 people. Mounted atop the structures were air defense platforms, one for observation, the other with fixed anti-aircraft guns. Each tower had walls of reinforced concrete that were six to eight feet thick; the structure itself was higher than a twelve-story building. The Zoo tower, built on the grounds of the Berlin Zoo, encompassed almost an entire city block. Within the structure were barracks, a hospital facility, two floors containing museum treasures (including Priam's Gold and the Pergamon Altar), kitchens, air-raid shelters, ammunition, and other equipment. Second in size was the Friedrichshain tower, located in the park of the same name, which housed the museums' four hundred plus paintings in addition to hundreds of sculptures, porcelain objects, almost two hundred cases of library books, and other antiquities.

By May 2 Russian soldiers controlled most of Berlin including the museum complex known as Museum Island. Despite the chaos, German museum officials, including none other than Dr. Kümmel, made contact with Russian officers on May 3 to discuss the posting of guards at the museums, and the Zoo and Friedrichshain towers. Although there was considerable damage to the museum buildings, the flak-towers were intact, even though they had taken direct hits from artillery shelling and bombing.

As of May 5 the priceless contents of Friedrichshain tower were unharmed. When German museum officials returned the next day for another check of its contents, a small fire on the first two floors of the flak-tower prevented access to the third and most important floor. By May 18, 1945, a much larger fire had consumed several other floors of the building, including those that contained the most important Berlin Museum paintings and sculpture. It was assumed then—and is still assumed today—that most if not all of the artwork stored there was destroyed by fire. There are several theories concerning the cause of the fires. Some believe the first and smaller fire was deliberately set to cover up looting by German civilians. Others believe Nazi SS officers were acting to deny the Russians possession of Germany's artistic patrimony. The larger fire may also have been the work of Nazi SS fanatics or, possible carelessness by guards who, lacking flashlights, would light bundled paper to illuminate the room, then drop it on the floor to extinguish it. It is but one mystery surrounding the events during the final days of the battle for Berlin.

Aachen was the first significant city in Germany occupied by Allied Forces. In the rubble of the streets, American GIs posted this sign with Hitler's ironic prophecy.

ITALY

Monte Cassino

After almost two months of intense fighting, the battle for Monte Cassino had become a stalemate. Considerable debate ensued among Allied commanders who were operating on the assumption—which later proved incorrect—that German forces had occupied the Abbey and were using it as an operational base. The resulting decision to bomb the Abbey, which occurred in February, 1944, succeeded in destroying the building but did not end the fighting, as German soldiers relocated to the bombed out structure to use it for protection. The battle would continue for three additional months and result in the deaths of more than 50,000 Allied and German soldiers. The fate of Monte Cassino would be endlessly discussed as to whether it should have been bypassed—or bombed—at the outset. Its destruction was a coup for German propaganda which took full advantage to characterize American forces as barbarians.

MFAA officers Lt. Col. Ernest T. DeWald and
Lt. Col. Ellis search for anything that can be
salvaged from the rubble of the Abbey.
In the photograph on the right, a headless
statue of St. Benedict still stands amid the
rubble as U.S. and Polish troops rest.
After the war, the Abbey was, once again,
reconstructed. Even the statues
were reassembled using the original
fragments (far right).

These photographs show the roofless Campo Santo as seen from above (to the right of the cathedral), and amidst its ruins.

Campo Santo

Campo Santo, Pisa's ancient cemetery, contains 12,192 square meters (40,000 square feet) of enclosed space with frescoes by various artists from the 14th and 15th centuries. This extraordinary building and its contents made it a "must-see" destination for visitors to Italy in the 19th and 20th centuries. When Capt. Deane Keller arrived he was appalled to discover a fire from the 40 days of fighting had melted the lead roof of Campo Santo and blistered the remaining frescoed walls (right). Capt. Keller's urgent action probably saved Campo Santo from complete ruin. He immediately brought to Pisa experts from Florence who recovered pieces of the shattered frescoes (opposite lower left) and secured those still attached. U.S. Army Engineers supervised the construction of scaffolding and a temporary roof to prevent further catastrophic damage. After his death in 1992, Capt. Deane Keller was honored by the citizens of Pisa and officials at Campo Santo by being laid to rest there.

September 1944

Leo von Klenze, *The Camposanto in Pisa*, 1858.

Oil on canvas,
103.5 × 130.5 cm
(40 ¾ × 51 ⅜ in).
Neue Pinakothek, Munich.

Florence

This pre-war photograph provides a magnificent view of the Ponte Santa Trinita.

The demolition of the Ponte Santa Trinita occurred on August 3, 1944.

Florentines used the remains of Ponte alle Grazie to cross the Arno River.

Blast damage created holes in the wall and ceiling of the third-floor corridor in the Uffizi Gallery.

FRANCE

Paris

Maj. Gen. Dietrich von Choltitz (above), German Commander of Paris, would later say: "It is always my lot to defend the rear of the German Army. And each time it happens I am ordered to destroy each city as I leave it." Even he had his limits; his decision to ignore Hitler's orders to destroy Paris saved the city from devastation.

The battle to liberate Paris was near. The Cathedral of Notre Dame (above left) was not damaged, but fighting took place directly in front of the church. This burned-out truck was abandoned by German troops fleeing the city.

Luxembourg Palace (left) was littered with equipment hastily abandoned by the German garrison in their retreat from the city.
August 1944

Rouen

Allied bombing destroyed this bridge in an effort to deter the German retreat. The great Cathedral of Rouen was severely damaged.

HOLLAND

The altar of this church in Panningen had been booby-trapped and mined. The retreating Nazis also destroyed the façade of the church. In this photograph an unidentified American GI speaks with a priest.

POLAND

"Berlin. Conference with the Führer. The Führer discussed the general situation with the Governor-General and approved the activity of the Governor-General in Poland, particularly in the demolition of the Warsaw Palace, the non-restoration of this city, and the evacuation of the art treasures.'"

<small>FIRST VOLUME OF HANS FRANK'S DIARY
EVIDENCE PRESENTED AT THE NUREMBERG TRIALS</small>

The Warsaw Castle was only partially damaged during the German invasion in 1939 (above). It was completely obliterated by German forces after the Warsaw Uprising in 1944. The photograph below shows the castle as it appears today.

Using Artworks to Rebuild

Bernardo Bellotto was an acclaimed painter known for the extraordinary degree of precision in his paintings of European cities. His works were so accurate that officials in Warsaw referenced his paintings to reconstruct buildings in their destroyed city. This Bellotto painting was used to rebuild the Church of the Sisters of the Blessed Sacrament, which was destroyed during the war. The photographs below show the church after the war, and as it appears today.

Bernardo Bellotto, *The Church of the Sisters of the Blessed Sacrament*, 1778.
Oil on canvas, 84 × 106 cm (33 × 41 ¾ in).
Royal Castle, Warsaw.

Warsaw

The Saxon Palace was completed in1842. In 1923, the monument to Prince Jozef Poniatowski was positioned in front of the colonnade. In 1925, the Tomb of the Unknown Soldier was enshrined beneath its arcade. In November 1944, German soldiers destroyed the Palace. By the hands of fate, only the section containing the Tomb of the Unknown Soldier survived. Rather than rebuild the Palace, Polish officials elected to use its remains as a memorial in the center of one of the city's beautiful parks.

OPPOSITE

The remains of a statue of Christ from the Holy Cross Church in Warsaw.

GERMANY

Berlin

The battered Reichstag, center of German government, as it was found by the 2nd U.S. Armored Division upon their occupation of the southwestern sector of the city. The wrecked vehicle in the foreground was once a part of the Red Army's massive invasion force that overran the city in early May, 1945.

Munich

Pfc. Lawrence W. Bartlett of Niagara Falls, New York, examines four fallen lions which once adorned the top of the Siegestor, built by King Ludwig I in 1844-52, in tribute to the Bavarian army.
June 1945

Frankfurt
An aerial view of the city in 1945.
Only the Cathedral was left standing.

Nuremberg

Daily life resumes. People carrying water buckets walk past two American GIs. In the distance, the twin spires of Lorenz Church still stand. On the right is a statue of Kaiser Wilhelm I.

1945

Dresden
This photograph was taken from the top of the "Rathaus," or town hall, overlooking the burned-out remains of the once beautiful city. In February, 1945, Allied bombing initiated a series of firestorms which caused devastating loss of life and destroyed the city.

The Flak-Towers in Berlin

The Zoo tower (above) was a fortress capable of sustaining up to 18,000 people. It was a city within a city. The Friedrichshain tower (right), only slightly smaller, housed the oversized paintings from the Berlin museums. Most of these works were destroyed when a fire consumed several floors of the building in May, 1945. In 1946 Allied Forces demolished all flak-towers. An anti-aircraft gun is still visible atop a turret (right).

TREASURES DESTROYED

Each of these masterpieces was among the more than four hundred paintings presumed destroyed by the fire in the Friedrichshain flak-tower.

Giovanni Bellini, *Madonna and Child*, c. 1490.
Panel. Gemäldegalerie,
Staatliche Museen zu Berlin (destroyed).

Andrea del Sarto, *Virgin and Child Enthroned With Eight Saints*, c. 1510-1530.
Oil on panel, 2.3 × 1.3 m (7 ft 6 in × 4 ft 1 in).
Gemäldegalerie, Staatliche Museen zu Berlin (destroyed).

Michelangelo Merisi da Caravaggio, *Saint Matthew and the Angel*, 1602.
Oil on canvas, 2.3 × 1.8 m (7 ft 7 in × 6 ft).
Gemäldegalerie, Staatliche Museen zu Berlin (destroyed).

Luca Signorelli,
***School of Pan*, c. 1496.**
Panel, 1.9 × 2.6 m
(6 ft 4 in × 8 ft 5 in).
Gemäldegalerie,
Staatliche Museen zu Berlin
(destroyed).

Peter Paul Rubens,
Bacchanal,
c. 1608-1619.
Oil on canvas,
2.1 × 2.7 m
(6 ft 11 in × 8 ft 9 in).
Gemäldegalerie,
Staatliche Museen zu
Berlin (destroyed).

EPILOGUE

Hitler, Göring, and other Nazi leaders invested an enormous amount of time building and then running recent history's most criminal enterprise. Had they spent as much time and effort on the war as they did assembling their art collections and planning for the museums that were to follow, one might wonder if the outcome would have been different. At least one of the principal war crime defendants on trial at Nuremberg in 1945 raised that point in the course of interviews conducted prior to sentencing.

The death of Hitler and other Nazi leaders, and the end of World War II, were only the beginning of a saga that continues today. Hundreds of thousands of objects looted by the Nazis remain missing. But the harmonic convergence of four events has created a realistic opportunity for closure of wounds that have been open for sixty years. The access and affordability of the Internet offer immediate contact with experts. The democracy of the Internet has eliminated the imbalance of access to information, and its anonymity may be the demise of those who have sequestered information that belongs in the public domain. It is only a matter of time.

Despite its extraordinary impact, the Internet cannot alone solve the problem. With the demise of communism, reunification of Germany, and the gradual opening of Eastern European countries, state records and other information is being revealed. This is an important development: the clues required to solve many of the unanswered questions will be found in documents and archival records removed from Germany by Red Army soldiers (and others). Some of these records are surely piled up in basements and warehouses. The influx of modern technology into Eastern Europe will enable better analysis and cataloging of such records as they are discovered.

Communism is being replaced by capitalism in all its forms. With the progressive development of laws governing business transactions—real property ownership in particular—and judicial systems established to resolve disputes, people in the Eastern countries are now enjoying activities taken for granted by those in the West: remodeling a home, restoring a dilapidated greenhouse, or building a second home. In the course of this new construction, walls will be knocked down, ground turned, and in some instances hidden artworks may be revealed.

The last ten years have also witnessed an explosion in the commercial value of art. It seems with each auction a new world record price is established. The attendant publicity has created a highly visible profile for art and, those who collect it. The escalating prices have created a tremendous incentive for people to sell—and for others, who are also profit-oriented—to locate lost or unclaimed paintings. Prior to the creation of the Internet, the private sale of artworks often occurred with buyer and seller making a minimal effort to check its background (or provenance). In fact, scrutiny has only become a priority in the past ten years or so—another example of the democracy of the Internet facilitating the flow of information and forcing certain established business practices to change.

Raphael, *Portrait of a Young Man*, 1516.
Oil on panel, 75 × 59 cm
(29 ½ × 23 ⅓ in).
Formerly in the Czartoryski
Collection, Cracow.
Stolen during World War II;
whereabouts unknown.

285

Art has, for better or worse, become a "big" business. The financial incentive for those persons with claims to pursue restitution has never been greater. The courts of choice reside in the United States, especially as a means of last resort when the claim involves a dispute with a foreign government. Some law firms have modified their practices to include advising clients on the pursuit of restitution claims, occasionally on a contingency basis. The hunt for "buried treasure" will also give rise to opportunists seeking to capitalize on the very lack of information that has impaired legitimate claimants from recovering art that once belonged to their family. For example, heirs of an owner who willingly sold a painting to a Nazi official or his agent prior to or during the war might now claim the sale occurred under duress. The claim alone could create unwelcome publicity and attention for the current owner. Money has changed the dynamics; it will continue to do so.

As time takes its inevitable toll, secrets will be revealed—some by choice, others by chance. Heirs will inherit items and in some cases, the problems that accompany them. Executors of estates will follow directives contained in wills and place merchandise for public sale only to discover a provenance problem. Such a finding may render the item unmarketable. Gradually, many of these missing artworks will surface, and in time find their way "home."

Foretelling the future is a perilous exercise but on this topic certain developments seem assured. Claims by heirs will increase dramatically. Some will be high profile, many will be settled privately. Eventually, the weight of claims and pressure from the court of public opinion will compel those remaining museums, private collectors, and dealers who have not already undertaken a thorough provenance analysis of works in their respective collections and inventories to do so. At this late stage there are no excuses.

Finally, discoveries will occur; some will be major news stories. Someday, a major work of art, such as the missing Raphael from Cracow or one or more of the Amber Panels, will either surface, or the way it met its demise will become known. Each such event will steer greater attention to other missing works. For those in possession of the missing artwork or knowledge of its whereabouts, pressure to come forward will increase. Twenty-five years from now it will be fair to assume that most of the remaining missing pieces were, in fact, destroyed. But what an interesting twenty-five years lies in wait.

THE RESCUE CONTINUES

July/August 2005

Altmann vs Austria: End in sight for long-running Nazi loot dispute

The long-running Maria Altmann Nazi-loot restitution case is to be submitted in Austria, the parties announced in May. Ms. Altmann is the niece and heir of Jewish sugar magnate Ferdinand Bloch-Bauer, whose art collection was stolen by Nazis in Vienna in 1938. She is claiming the return of six paintings by Gustave Klimt that had belonged to her uncle, from the Republic of Austria. The works have been valued at roughly $150 million.

May 2005

Norton Museum's war loot research grant

The Norton Museum of Art has received a $50,000 grant to fund research for European paintings, the provenance of which is incomplete or the ownership of which had changed hands in Nazi-occupied Europe.

April 2005

Israel Museum returns Degas drawing to dealer's heir

The Israel Museum has returned a Degas drawing to the daughter-in-law of Jacques Goudstikker, the Dutch dealer who died while fleeing the Nazi occupation in May 1940.

March 2005

Claim to Liz Taylor's Van Gogh is dismissed

A federal court here has thrown out a claim against the actress Elizabeth Taylor seeking a painting by Van Gogh, which the claimants broadly asserted was lost to Nazi persecution without, however, claiming that it ever fell into Nazi hands.

March 2005

Putin's policy shift

Just a few weeks after German Culture Minister, Christina Weiss, said she would continue to lobby Russia for the return of art taken from Germany by Soviet troops during World War II, Russian President Vladimir Putin, has made a surprisingly conciliatory gesture.

February 2005

Soviet Loot to go on show for first time

Art stolen from Hungarian Jews in World War II will be displayed in September.

The state Nizhny Novgorod Art Museum has announced that it is to hold an exhibition of art looted from Hungary by Soviet troops in 1945, none of which has been seen since.

December 2004

Rubens looted from Germany discovered at Hermitage

A painting by Rubens, "Venus disarming Mars" (1615-20), once in the collection of the Rheinsberg Palace, Berlin, and believed to have been looted by Soviet troops from the Konigsberg Castle, East Prussia in 1945, has been found by scholars in the State Hermitage Museum in St. Petersburg.

December 2004

War provenance art: a growing source of supply in the market

Christie's follows Sotheby's and appoints a director of restitution.

It is impossible to estimate the value of cultural assets looted in the period from 1933 to 1948; apart from the monetary value, the emotional cost to families who lost possessions cannot be measured on any scale.

However, there is one figure that can be quantified: that of the amount of restituted art sold at public auction. Since 1996, Sotheby's and Christie's alone have sold a combined total of about $252 million of art returned to families from museums and private collections. As more and more art, primarily looted by the Nazis as well as the Red Army, is being identified and returned, it is becoming an increasingly important source of supply for the auction houses. And because it is generally the heirs of the original owners who receive the restituted art, they often have to sell in order to share equitably the value of the works, particularly in the case of major paintings.

September 2004

Ukraine returns Koenigs' drawings

A group of 139 looted Old Master drawings has been returned from the Ukraine to the Netherlands, and is on display at Rotterdam's Boijmans Van Beuningen Museum. The works are mostly by 15th- and 16th-century German artists, including Holbein, but there is also a Jacopo de' Barbari still-life of a dead jay. It was not until 1998 that they were discovered in the basement store of the Khanenko Museum in Kiev.

The drawings were once part of a larger group of 528 works belonging to collector Franz Koenigs which was seized in Rotterdam by Hitler's art agent, Hans Posse, in 1940.

June 2004

Settlement, not litigation is the way forward

The Musée des Beaux-Arts of Strasbourg is seeking funds to compensate the heirs of the Jewish owner of a Canaletto painting in its collection which was recently identified as having been looted by the Nazis in Vienna after Austrian annexation in 1938.

The painting, on copper, is just one of four Canaletto paintings that Nazis stole from Bernhard Altmann, a Viennese cashmere sweater manufacturer, when they confiscated his entire estate in 1938 after he had fled to London.

May 2004

Looted Viennese Old Masters on sale in Moscow

The Art Newspaper can reveal that two paintings looted from Austria's Academy of Fine Arts at the end of World War II have turned up, apparently for sale, in Moscow. The Dutch Old Masters are still lifes by Willem van Aelst (1660s) and Rachel Ruysch (1703). Both had been bequeathed to the Academy in 1822 and were among a group of pictures sent for safe-keeping during the war to Heiligenkreuz Abbey, 20 kilometres south of Vienna. The abbey served as a billet for Soviet troops in 1945 and the Ruysch and Van Aelst are assumed to have been looted by Red Army soldiers.

October 2003

Website to help in the search for Nazi loot in US museum collections

A new website has been set up to facilitate searches for Nazi-looted works of art that may be in the collections of US museums. The American Association of Museums (AAM) has launched the Nazi-Era Provenance Internet Portal, a central registry of works in US museum collections which changed or could have changed hands in Europe from 1933 to 1945.

July 2003

Austrian museum restitutes Schiele which sells for £12.6 million

A landscape by Egon Schiele, stolen by the Nazis in WWII, set a world record for a restituted work of art and a new artist's record at Sotheby's in London on June 23, when it sold for £12.6 million ($21 million). "Krumau Landscape", 1916, had spent the last 50 years in the Neue Galerie, Linz (coincidentally Hitler's birthplace), after the gallery had bought it without realizing it had been stolen from the original Jewish owners.

May 2002

German museums commit themselves to provenance research

Germany's museums are finally trying to come to terms with one of the darkest chapters of their history: the acquisition of works of art looted during the Nazi period 1933-45.

January 2002

Top museums face claims for Dürers

Twelve major museums in Europe and North America are resisting claims for the return of Dürer drawings which were looted during WWII from the Lubomirski Museum in Lvov, a city previously in Poland and now in the Ukraine. At the end of the war the important collection of 24 Dürers was found in an Austrian salt mine and in 1950 it was handed over by the Americans to the Lubomirski family, rather than returned to Lvov.

The Amber Room

In 1716, King Frederick William I of Germany made a gift of the Amber Room to Peter the Great. Each piece of the translucent brownish-yellow fossil was painstakingly hand-carved and fitted by German master craftsmen over the course of twelve years.

The invading Nazis looted the panels in late 1940 and shipped them to Königsberg Castle. They survived Allied bombing in August 1944 and were about to be shipped to Saxony in January 1945 when Soviet forces stormed Königsberg. Some believe the panels were destroyed in the subsequent battle; others believe that the panels were buried or otherwise hidden. Even today treasure hunters are digging into abandoned tunnels and mine shafts in search of these extraordinary treasures.

The photograph above is taken from a color daguerreotype of the early 20 century; it is the only known color reproduction of the Amber Room prior to its theft. The photograph on the right shows the fully reconstructed Amber Room in all its splendor.

SOURCES

FRONT MATTER

ii *"Anyone who sees and paints a sky green and pastures blue ought to be sterilized."*
Adolf Hitler
Public Domain

vi *"Art is a human activity, having as its aim to convey to people the highest and best feelings up to which mankind has lived..."*
Leo Tolstoy
What is Art?, translated by Charles Johnston (Philadelphia: Henry Altemus, 1898), p. 99.

viii *"Humanity looks to works of art to shed light upon its path and its destiny."*
Pope John Paul II
"Pope John Paul II, 1920-2005," *The Art Newspaper*, no. 158 (May 2005), p. 4.

x *"...The purpose of the people of America that the freedom of the human spirit and human mind which has produced the world's great art and all its science—shall not be utterly destroyed."*
President Franklin D. Roosevelt
National Gallery of Art, Gallery Archives, Washington, D.C.

xi *"All things beautiful and mortal pass, but not art."* (cosa bella e mortal passa e non d'arte).
Leonardo da Vinci
Jean Paul Richter, ed., trans., *The Literary Works of Leonardo da Vinci*, (London: S. Low, Marston, Searle and Rivington, 1883).

xvi *"Time and again during the two and a half centuries of our national existence, our political and intellectual leaders as well as our Average American have crossed the seas to make intimate, first-hand contact with the surviving evidences of past cultures and to draw renewed inspiration there from. No amount of book knowledge by itself can equal the experience of actual contact or association."*
Lt. Col. Ernest T. DeWald, Monuments Officer
Henry La Farge ed., *Lost Treasures of Europe* (New York: Pantheon Books, 1946), p. 8.

CHAPTER 1: SETTING THE STAGE

5 *"I observed his face. It was grave, solemn, yet brimming with revenge. There was also in it, as in his springy step, a note of the triumphant conqueror, the defier of the world. There was something else, difficult to describe, in his expression, a sort of scornful inner joy at being present at this great reversal of fate—a reversal he himself had wrought."*
William Shirer
Berlin Diary: The Journal of a Foreign Correspondent (Northwalk, CT: Easton Press, 1940), pp. 420-21. Reprinted by permission of Don Congdon Associates, Inc., ©1941, renewed 1968 by William Shirer.

9 *"To whom should propaganda be addressed? To the scientifically trained intelligentsia or to the less educated masses? It must be addressed always and exclusively to the masses.... The art of propaganda lies in understanding the emotional ideas of the great masses and finding...the way to the attention and thence to the heart of the broad masses."*
Adolf Hitler
Mein Kampf, translated by Ralph Manheim, (New York: Houghton Mifflin Company, 1943), p. 179.

9 *"Propaganda must not serve the truth especially insofar as it might bring out something favorable for the opponent."*
Adolf Hitler
Mein Kampf, p. 182, as cited in Donald O. Bolander, ed., *Instant Quote Dictionary* (New Jersey: Career Institute, 1969), p. 212.

9 *"The crowd will finally succeed in remembering only the simplest concepts repeated a thousand times."*
Adolf Hitler
Mein Kampf, p. 185, as cited in Martin Gray and A. Norman Jeffares, eds., *A Dictionary of Quotations* (New York: Barnes & Noble Books, 1995), p. 323.

9 *"We call upon our artists to wield the noblest weapon in the defense of the German people: German Art!"*
Adolf Hitler
Remarks made at a Nuremberg Rally, August, 1933, as cited in *Temple of German Art* (Nazi Art Publication), p. 3.

9 *"The Führer loves art because he himself is an artist. Under his blessed hand a Renaissance has begun."*
Joseph Goebbels
Degenerate Art, VHS, (David Grubin Productions, Inc. and the Los Angeles County Museum of Art, 1993).

9 *"...One day it became clear to me that I would become a painter, an artist...My father was struck speechless...'Artist! No! Never as long as I live!' ... My father would never depart from his 'Never!' and I intensified my 'Nevertheless!'"*
Adolf Hitler
Mein Kampf, Manheim trans., pp 9-10.

12 *"The broad mass of a people...falls victim to a big lie more easily than to a small one."*
Adolf Hitler
Mein Kampf, p. 231, as cited in Gray and Jeffares, p. 323.

12 *"Tutti questi quadri... All these pictures...."*
Benito Mussolini
Lynn Nicholas, *The Rape of Europa: The Fate of Europe's Treasues in the Third Reich and the Second World War* (New York: Vintage Books, 1995), p.42

12 *"He [Hitler] never stopped expressing his joy that the visits to Rome and Florence had made it possible to admire immortal masterpieces that he had previously known only from photographs."*
Christa Schroeder
Frederick Spotts, *Hitler and the Power of Aesthetics* (Woodstock, NY: The Overlook Press, 2002), p. 189.

12 *"Masterpieces of theatrical art." "I had spent six years in St. Petersburg before the war in the best days of the old Russian ballet," "but for grandiose beauty I have never seen a ballet to compare with it."*
British Ambassador Sir Nevile Henderson
Alan Bullock, *Hitler: A Study in Tyranny* (London: Odhams Books Limited, Lond Acre, 1952), p. 379.

14 *"In the evening the people's will power more easily succumbs to the dominating force of a stronger will."*
Joseph Goebbels
Unknown

16 *"If we use them in such large numbers for a thing like this, other countries will think we're swimming in searchlights," commented Hitler. Speer later wrote: "The actual effect far surpassed anything I had imagined. The hundred and thirty sharply defined beams,*

placed around the field at intervals of forty feet, were visible to a height of twenty five thousand feet, after which they merged into a general glow. The feeling was of a vast room, with the beams serving as mighty pillars of infinitely high outer walls. Now and then a cloud moved though this wreath of light, bringing an element of surrealistic surprise to the mirage. I imagined that this "cathedral of light" was the first luminescent architecture of this type, and for me it remains not only my most beautiful architectural concept but after its fashion, the only one which has survived the passage of time."

Albert Speer
Albert Speer, *Inside the Third Reich, Memoirs,* translated by Richard and Clara Winston (New York: The Macmillan Company, 1970), pp. 58-59.

16 *"But the masses are slow moving, and they always require a certain time before they are ready even to notice a thing, and only after the simplest ideas are repeated thousands of times will the masses finally remember them...."*

Adolf Hitler
Mein Kampf, Manheim trans., p.185.

17 *"...And then, to our amazement, we shall see what tremendous results such perseverance leads to...results that are almost beyond our understanding."*

Adolf Hitler
Mein Kampf, Manheim trans., p.185.

18 *"As our leader saved the German people from the threatening chaos of Bolshevism, so he also protected the German soul above all; however, there was a fall and degeneration of German Art. With the "house of German art" he created a metropolis for the German artists which will henceforth protect our people... with a new healthy opinion of art with its natural and clear view of life.... German art is again healthy."*

Heinrich Hoffmann
"Introduction," *Kunst Dem Volk* (April 20, 1943).

19 *" 'Works of art' that are not capable of being understood in themselves but need some pretentious instruction book to justify their existence-until at long last they find someone sufficiently browbeaten to endure such stupid or impudent twaddle with patience-will never again find their way to the German people."*

Adolf Hitler
Stephanie Barron, ed., *"Degenerate Art," The Fate of the Avant-Garde in Nazi Germany,* exh. cat. (Los Angeles: Los Angeles County Museum of Art, 1991), p. 376.

27 *"Paintings from the degenerate art auction will now be offered on the international art market. In so doing we hope at least to make some money from this garbage."*

Joseph Goebbels
Elke Fröhlich, ed., *Die Tagebücher von Joseph Goebbels* (Munich: K G Saur, 1987), part 1, vol. 3, entry for July 29, 1938.

36 *"Herewith I am commissioning Herr Galeriedirektor Director of the Museum/Gallery Dr. Hans Posse, to build the new art museum in Linz-Donau. All Party and government officials are obliged to support Dr. Posse with the completion of this order."*

Adolf Hitler
Führer's Favorite Museum, after p. 96, translated by Sabine Ranft.

CHAPTER 2: PREPARATIONS

47 *"It was in the face of this appalling prospect that we had been charged, for the first time in our history, with the securing of the national artistic inheritance. Whatever the threats which weighed on its inhabitants, France was above all to save the spiritual values which it held as an integral part of its heart and its culture. To put at shelter its works of art, its archives, its libraries, was indeed one of the first reflexes of defense of our country."*

Rose Valland
Le Front de l'Art 1939-1945 (Paris: Librarie Plon, 1961), p. 8.

47 *"Bury them in caves or cellars, but not a picture shall leave these islands."*
Prime Minister Sir Winston Churchill
Neil MacGregor, "How Titian helped the war effort," *The Times* (June 5, 2004).

55 *"The statue rocked onto an inclined wooden ramp, held back by two groups of men, who controlled her descent with ropes stretched to either side...the Victory rolled slowly forward, her stone wings trembling slightly."*
Nicholas, *The Rape of Europa*:p. 54, as translated from M. Hours, *Une Vie au Louvre* (Paris, 1987), p. 44.

83 *"It is for this reason that the people of America accept the inheritance of these ancient arts. Whatever these paintings may have been to men who looked at them a generation back—today they are not only works of art. Today they are the symbols of the human spirit, and of the world the freedom of the human spirit made—a world against which armies now are raised and countries overrun and men imprisoned and their work destroyed. To accept, today, the work of German painters such as Holbein and Dürer and of Italians like Botticelli and Raphael, and of painters of the low countries like Van Dyck and Rembrandt, and of famous Frenchmen, famous Spaniards—to accept this work today on behalf of the people of this democratic nation is to assert the belief of the people of this nation in a human spirit which now is everywhere endangered and which, in many countries where it first found form and meaning, has been rooted out and broken and destroyed. To accept this work today is to assert the purpose of the people of America that the freedom of the human spirit and human mind which has produced the world's great art and all its science—shall not be utterly destroyed."*
President Franklin D. Roosevelt.
National Gallery of Art, Gallery Archives, Washington, D.C.

CHAPTER 3: WAR ARRIVES

87 *"The destruction of Poland has priority...even if war breaks out in the West, the destruction of Poland remains the priority...I shall give a propagandist reason for starting the war no matter whether it is plausible or not. The victor will not be asked afterwards whether he told the truth or not. When starting and waging war, it is not right that matters but victory. Close your hearts to pity. Act brutally."*
Adolf Hitler
Bullock, p. 527.

87 *"...We shall seek no terms, we shall tolerate no parley; we may show mercy—we shall ask for none."*
Prime Minister Sir Winston Churchill
"The War of the Unknown Warriors," speech, BBC Broadcast, London, July 14, 1940.

88 *"The Führer has decided to erase from the face of the earth St. Petersburg. The existence of this large city will have no further interest after Soviet Russia is destroyed... It is proposed to approach near to the city and to destroy it with the aid of an artillery barrage from weapons of different calibers and long air attacks... The problem of the life of the population and the provisioning of them is a problem which cannot and must not be decided by us. In this war...we are not interested in preserving even a part of the population of this large city."*
Hitler's orders through the Chief of Naval Staff
Trial of the Major War Criminals before the International Military Tribunal, Nuremberg, November 14, 1945-October 1, 1946 (Nuremberg, 1947), vol. 1, p. 58, exhibit no. USSR-113. (Hereafter referred to as *Nuremberg Trials*).

96 *"This is the finest moment of my life."*
Adolf Hitler
Robert Wernick, *World War II: Blitzkrieg* (New York: Time-Life Books, 1976), p. 196.

CHAPTER 4: THEFT BY ANY OTHER NAME

105 *"We now have to face the task of cutting up the cake according to our needs in order to be able: first, to dominate it; second, to administer it; third, to exploit it."*

Adolf Hitler
Robert Edwin Herzstein, *World War II: The Nazis* (Alexandria: Time Life Books, 1980), p. 107.

105 *"My pictures, in the collections which I have bought in the course of years, have never been collected for private purposes, but only for the extension of a gallery in my home town of Linz a.d. Donau."*
Adolf Hitler
Douglas Brinkley, ed., "My Private Will and Testament," in *The New York Times Living History. World War II: The Allied Counteroffensive, 1942-1945* (New York: Times Books, 2003), p. 332.

105 *"It exploitation used to be called plundering. But today things have become more humane. In spite of that, I intend to plunder, and to do it thoroughly."*
Hermann Göring
Herzstein, p. 107.

107 *"They...tried to paint a picture of me as a looter of art treasures. In the first place, during a war everybody loots a little bit...*
Hermann Göring
Robert Gellately, ed., *The Nuremberg Interviews* (New York: Alfred A. Knopf, 2004), pp. 128-29.

111 *"I was able to gain some knowledge on the public and private collections, as well as clerical property, in Cracow and Warsaw. It is true that we cannot hope too much to enrich ourselves from the acquisition of great art works of paintings and sculptures, with exception of the Veit Stoss altar and the plates of Hans von Kulmbach in the Church of Maria in Cracow...and several other works from the National Museum in Warsaw."*
Hans Posse
Nuremberg Trials, vol. 1, p. 243.

114 *"On Wednesday, 5 February 1941, I was ordered to the Jeu de Paume by the Reich Marshal. At 1500 o'clock, the Reich Marshal, accompanied by General Hanesse, Herr Angerer, and Herr Hofer, visited the exhibition of Jewish art treasures newly set up there.... Then with me as his guide, the Reich Marshal inspected the exhibited art treasures and made a selection of those works of art which were to go to the Führer, and those which were to be placed in his own collection. During this confidential conversation, I again called the Reich Marshal's attention to the fact that a note of protest had been received from the French Government against the activity of the Einstazstab Rosenberg, with reference to the Hague Rules on Land Warfare recognized by Germany at the Armistice of Compiègne and I pointed out that General Von Stülpnagel's interpretation of the manner in which the confiscated Jewish art treasures are to be treated, was apparently contrary to the Reich Marshal's interpretation. Thereupon, the Reich Marshal asked for a detailed explanation and gave the following orders: 'First, it is my orders that you have to follow. You will act directly according to my orders. The art collected in the Jeu de Paume is to be loaded on a special train immediately and taken to Germany by order of the Reich Marshal. These art objects which are to go in the Führer's possession, and those art objects which the Reich Marshal claims for himself, will be loaded on two railroad cars which will be attached to the Reich Marshal special trains, and upon his departure for Germany, at the beginning of next week, will be taken along to Berlin. Feldführer Von Behr will accompany the Reich Marshal in his special train on the journey to Berlin.' When I made the objection that the jurists would probably be of different opinion and that protests would most likely be made by the military commander in France, the Reich Marshal answered, saying verbatim as follows, 'Dear Bunjes let me worry about that; I am the highest jurist in the State.' The Reich Marshal promised to send from his headquarters by courier to the Chief of the Military Administrative District of Paris on Thursday, 6 February, the written order for the transfer to Germany of the confiscated Jewish art treasures."*
Dr. Bunjes
Nuremberg Trials, vol. 9, p. 547-49.

116 *"The confiscation of Jewish homes was carried out as follows: When no records were available of the addresses of Jews who had*

fled or departed, as was the case, for instance, in Paris, so-called requisitioning officials went from house to house in order to collect information as to abandoned Jewish homes. They drew up inventories of these homes and sealed them. In Paris alone, about twenty requisitioning officials requisitioned more than 38,000 homes. The transportation of these homes were completed with all the available vehicles of the Union of Parisian Moving Contractors who had to provide up to 150 trucks, and 1,200 to 1,500 laborers daily."
Rosenberg Report
Nuremberg Trials, vol. 9, p. 88.

117 *"'52,828 Jewish lodgings were seized and sealed in favor of the bombed-out victims meaning homeless Germans. Including special orders, furniture has been removed from 47,569 dwellings for shipment to the bombed cities'... 69,619 Jewish lodging were looted, that the furniture occupied over 1 million cubic meters, and that it took 26,984 freight cars, that is 674 trains, to remove it."*
Rosenberg Report
Nuremberg Trials, vol. 11, pp. 58-59.

117 *"It is quite true that I received a governmental order to confiscate archives, works of art, and later, household goods from Jewish citizens in France... The suggestion for these measures was given only when I was informed that the Jewish people in question no longer inhabited their institutions, castles, and apartments-that they had left Paris and other places and had not returned."*
Alfred Rosenberg
Nuremberg Trials, vol. 11, pp. 58-59.

124 *"At Zarskoje Selo the company seized and secured the property belonging to the palace-museum of the Empress Catherine. The Chinese silk draperies and the carved gilt ornaments were torn from the walls. The floor of artistic ornaments was dismantled and taken away. From the palace of the Emperor Alexander antique furniture and a large library containing some 6,000 to 7,000 volumes in French and over 5,000 volumes and manuscripts in Russian, were removed... 'After the occupation of any big city, the leaders of these kommandos arrive, accompanied by various art experts. They inspect museums, picture galleries, exhibitions, and institutions of art and culture, they determine their condition and confiscate everything of value.'"*
Rosenberg Report
Nuremberg Trials, vol. 7, p. 64.

125 *"The Army is interested in extinguishing fires only in such buildings as may be used for Army billets... All the rest to be destroyed; no historical or artistic buildings in the East to be of any value whatsoever."*
Order issued by Field Marshall Walter Von Reichenau and approved by Hitler
Nuremberg Trials, vol. 8, p. 64.

CHAPTER 5: HEROES AND HEROINES

127 *"Prior to this war, no army had thought of protecting the monuments of the country in which and with which it was at war, and there were no precedents to follow.... All this was changed by a general order issued by the Supreme Commander-in-chief General Eisenhower just before he left Algiers, an order accompanied by a personal letter to all Commanders...the good name of the Army depended in great measure on the respect which it showed to the art heritage of the modern world."*
Lt. Col. Sir Leonard Woolley, Monuments Officer
Lord Methuen, *Normandy Diary* (London: Robert Hale Limited, 1952), p. xv.

127 *"Shortly we will be fighting our way across the continent of Europe.... Inevitably, in the path of our advance will be found historical monuments and cultural centers which symbolize to the world all that we are fighting to preserve. It is the responsibility of every commander to protect and respect these symbols whenever possible."*

General Dwight D. Eisenhower
National Archives and Records Administration, College Park, MD.

128 *"…A corps of specialists to deal with the matter of protecting monuments and works of art in liaison with the Army and Navy."*

Henry Francis Taylor
Nicholas, *The Rape of Europa*, p. 211, as cited from National Archives and Records Administration, RG 239/53.

136 *"We are a conquering army…not a pillaging army."*

Lt. Gen. Omar Bradley
National Archives and Records Administration, College Park, MD.

150 *"It Major Balfour's death is a great and unexpected blow. He had written only the day before, so cheerfully, delighted with being at the front; then he was killed in action, where actually engaged in saving some of those works of art which he loved so much. He had done wonderfully good work, as those who knew him knew he would do; he leaves a gap in our service which no one will be able to fill so well. The whole field of art history has suffered a tragic loss."*

Lt. Col. Sir Leonard Woolley, Monuments Officer
Kings College Archives Centre, Cambridge, *The Papers of Ronald Edmund Balfour*, Misc. 5.

150 *"Fragments of two large 16th century retables altarpieces of carved and painted wood have been collected and removed to safety. Parish archives found in a blasted safe and strewn over the floor of the wrecked sacristy have also been removed for safekeeping"*

Major Ronald E. Balfour, Monuments Officer
Kings College Archives Centre, Cambridge, *The Papers of Ronald Edmund Balfour*, Misc. 5.

151 *"The American Commission has learned with the deepest regret of the death of your son Captain Walter Huchthausen. Captain Huchthausen was, in the opinion of this Commission, one of the outstanding Monuments Officers in the field, and his work in the Valley of the Loire and at Aachen will remain as a signal contribution to the cultural preservation of Europe. His knowledge of Germany made him uniquely fitted for the work there and his loss is an irreparable one."*

David E. Finley
Harvard University Archives

CHAPTER 6: TREASURE FOUND

153 *"We followed him the miner into the unlighted mine chamber. Flashlights supplemented the wavering flames of the miner's lamps. Ahead of us we could make out row after row of high packing cases. Beyond them was a broad wooden platform. The rays of our flashlights revealed a bulky object resting on the center of the platform. We came closer. We could see that it was a statue, a marble statue, and then we knew—it was Michelangelo's Madonna from Bruges, one of the world's great masterpieces."*

Lt. Cdr. Thomas Carr Howe, Jr., Monuments Officer
Thomas Howe, *Salt Mines and Castles* (New York: The Bobbs-Merrill Company, 1946), p. 142.

179 *"According to this report, 21,903 objects taken from 203 private collections, were removed, notably from the Rothschild, Alphons Kahn, David Weil, Lévy de Benzion, and the Seligmann brothers collections. According to the same report there were 'all told, 29 transports, 137 trucks, and 4,174 cases.'"*

Dr. Scholz
Nuremberg Trials, vol. 7, p. 63.

196 *"The light of our lamps played over the soft folds of the Madonna's robe, the delicate modeling of her face. Her grave eyes looked down, seemed only half aware of the sturdy Child nestling close against her, one hand firmly held in hers."*

Lt. Cdr. Thomas Carr Howe, Jr., Monuments Officer
Howe, pp. 142-43.

CHAPTER 7: COLLECTING POINTS

207 *"It was sort of like running a movie backwards; all the trainloads that had gone to Germany and to the mines and whatever now started coming back. Truckload after truckload and plane loads went back to Belgium, France, Italy…Once the works got there, committees in those countries were organized to decide who they belonged to and who should get them back, which became a very controversial issue."*

Lynn Nicholas
Interview, March 15, 2005, from *The Rape of Europa* (Actual Films, 2006).

222 *"I would walk into the loose document room to take a look at the things there and find it impossible to tear myself away from the fascinating pile of letters, folders and little personal bundles. Not that what you held in your hand was so engrossing, but rather what the next intriguing item might be. Or, in the sorting room I would come to a box of books which the sorters had brought together into one fold…books from a library which once had been in some distant town in Poland, or an extinct Yeshiva. There was something sad and mournful about these volumes…as if they were whispering a tale of yearning and hope long since obliterated.*

I would pick up a badly worn Talmud with hundreds of names of many generations of students and scholars. Where were they now? Or, rather where were their ashes? In what incinerator were they destroyed? I would find myself straightening out these books and arranging them in the boxes with a personal sense of tenderness as if they had belonged to someone dear to me, someone recently deceased.

There were thousands of loose family photographs without any identification. How dear all these tokens of love and gentle care must have been to someone and now they were so useless, destined to be burned, buried, or thrown away. All these things made my blood boil…How difficult it is to look at the contents of the depot with the detachment of someone evaluating property or with the impersonal view-point of scholarly evaluation."

Capt. Isaac Bencowitz, Monuments Officer
Walter I. Farmer, *The Safekeepers: A Memoir of the Arts at the End of World War II* (New York: Walter de Gruyter, 2000), p. 100, as cited in Leslie L. Poste, "Books Go Home From the Wars," *Library Journal* (December 1, 1948), p. 1703.

CHAPTER 8: HOMEWARD BOUND

227 *"…No historical grievance will rankle so long, or be the cause of so much justified bitterness, as the removal, for any reason, of a part of the heritage of any nation, even if that heritage may be interpreted as a prize of war. And though this removal may be done with every intention of altruism, we are none the less convinced that it is our duty, individually and collectively, to protest against it, and that though our obligations are to the nation to which we owe allegiance, there are yet further obligation to common justice, decency, and the establishment of the power of right, not of expediency or might, among civilized nations."*

"Wiesbaden Manifesto"
Farmer, p. 147.

227 *"Stalin rose and gripped the back of his chair with such force that his brown hands went white at the knuckles. He spat out his words as if they burnt his mouth. Great stretches of his country had been laid to waste, he said, and the peasants put to the sword. Reparations should be paid to the countries that had suffered most. While he was speaking, nobody moved."*

Harry Hopkins
Earl F. Ziemke, *World War II: The Soviet Juggernaut* (Alexandria: Time Life Books, 1980), p. 186.

229 *"…The Moscow reparation commission should take in its initial studies as a basis for discussion the suggestion of the Soviet Government that the total sum of the reparation…should be $22 billion dollars equivalent to $230 billion dollars in 2004 and that 50 per cent should go to the Union of Soviet Socialist Republics."*

Yalta Conference
The Avalon Project at Yale Law School, www.yale.edu/lawweb/aval-on/wwii/yalta.htm

229 "...Equipment, machine tools, ships, rolling stock, German investments abroad, shares of industrial, transport and other enterprises in Germany, etc., these removals to be carried out chiefly for the purpose of destroying the war potential of Germany."

Yalta Conference
The Avalon Project at Yale Law School, www.yale.edu/lawweb/aval-on/wwii/yalta.htm

229 "Here lie Leningraders, Here lie citizens—men, women and children. Beside them lie Red Army soldiers. They defended you with their lives, Leningrad, the cradle of the Revolution. We would not be able to give their noble names here for so many of them lie under the ever-lasting guard of granite. Looking at these stones, remember: no one has been forgotten and nothing has been forgotten. The enemy, clad in armour and iron, was forcing its way into the city. But workers, schoolchildren, teachers, civil guards stood up together with the army, and said, all as one: sooner death will be scared by us than we will be scared by death. We have not forgotten the famine-stricken, ferocious, dark winter of forty-one—forty-two, nor the fierce bombardments and savage bombings of forty-three. The entire city land had been pierced. None of your lives, comrades, have been forgotten. Under continuous fire from the sky, land and water you performed your everyday feat simply and with dignity. And together with the fatherland you all have gained the victory. So let the grateful people, the Motherland and the hero-city of Leningrad forever bow down their banners to your immortal lives in this field of solemn sorrow."

Piskariovskoye Memorial Cemetery
Translated by Sergei Beck.

236 "All works of art for whose fate we still tremble will return to us, bringing the light of their beauty to attract, as before, pilgrims from every country and to inspire thoughts of peace."

Dr. Cesare Fasola
Cesare Fasola, *The Florence Galleries and the War* (Florence: Casa Editrice Monsalvato, 1945), p. 75.

240 "The large painting was the Three Graces, painted by Rubens was too large to fit in the standard closed freight car, so we made a special tight plywood box, lined with waterproof paper, insulated it against frost with excelsior padding, and shipped it on a flat-car. When completed, the crate measured 2.75 meters square by 30 centimeters thick 9 feet × 1 foot. A scaffold of heavy planks was constructed on the flatcar and the crate was set upright on edge and lashed securely to this framework. Even then we had to slope the scaffold 30 degrees in order to clear tunnels. After the crate was in place it was covered by two heavy tarpaulins."

Maj. Edward E. Adams
"Looted Art Treasures Go Back to France," *The Quartermaster Review* (Sept.-Oct. 1946).

252 "In September, pets were still a customary attribute of the prewar life. In October, their number noticeably reduced and by winter, they totally disappeared."

Vladimir Nitkitin
Disguised Blockade: Leningrad 1941-1944 (Leipzig: Limbus Press, 2002), p. 82. Translated by Sergei Beck.

253 "We are barbarians and we wish to be barbarians. It is an honorable calling."

Adolf Hitler
Nuremberg Trials, vol. 8, p. 53.

256 "My dear Marshal Stalin: I am sending to you two scrolls for Stalingrad and Leningrad, which cities have won the wholehearted admiration of the American people. The heroism of the citizens of these two cities and the soldiers who so ably defended them has not only been an inspiration to the people of the United States, but has served to bind even more closely the friendship of our two nations. Stalingrad and Leningrad have become synonyms for the fortitude and endurance which has enabled us to resist and will finally enable us to overcome the aggression of our enemies. I hope that in presenting these scrolls to the two cities you will see fit to convey to their citizens my own personal expressions of friendship and admiration and my hope that our people will continue to develop that close understanding which has marked our common effort. Very sincerely yours, Franklin D. Roosevelt"

President Franklin D. Roosevelt
Franklin D. Roosevelt Library, Washington, D.C.

257 "... Sooner Death will be Scared by Us..."
Piskariovskoye Memorial Cemetery
Translated by Sergei Beck.

CHAPTER 9: CASUALTIES OF WAR

259 "Germany will either be a world power or will not exist at all."
Adolf Hitler
Mein Kampf, p. 654, as cited in Gray and Jeffares, p. 323.

259 "If the war is to be lost, the nation also will perish. This fate is inevitable. There is no need to consider the basis even of a most primitive existence any longer. On the contrary, it is better to destroy even that, and to destroy ourselves. The nation has proved itself weak, and the future belongs solely to the stronger eastern nation. Besides, those who remain after the battle are of little value; for the good have fallen."
Adolf Hitler
Nuremberg Trials, vol. 41, p. 430, and vol. 16, p. 500, as cited in Bullock, pp. 774-75.

260 "...must be utterly destroyed. On the departure of the Wermacht, nothing must be left standing, no church, no artistic monument."
Adolf Hitler
Martin Blumenson, *World War II: Liberation* (Alexandria: Time Life Books, 1980), p. 132.

260 "...ruined city may be a prey to epidemics."
Adolf Hitler
Blumenson, p. 132.

260 "Paris must not fall into the hands of the enemy except as a field of ruins."
Adolf Hitler
Blumenson, p. 132.

260 "Before and during battle a historic monument was no more sacred to the Germans than any military installation. Again and again they used church towers as observation posts, and snipers fired from them at our advancing troops."
Capt. James Rorimer, Monuments Officer
James J. Rorimer, *Survival: The Salvage and Protection of Art in War* (New York: Abelard Press, 1950), p. 1.

268 "It is always my lot to defend the rear of the German Army. And each time it happens I am ordered to destroy each city as I leave it."
Maj. Gen. Dietrich von Choltitz
Blumenson, p. 132.

272 "Berlin. Conference with the Führer. The Führer discussed the general situation with the Governor-General and approved the activity of the Governor-General in Poland, particularly in the demolition of the Warsaw Palace, the non-restoration of this city, and the evacuation of the art treasures.'"
Hans Frank
Nuremberg Trials, vol. 8, p. 64.

CREDITS

NOTE ABOUT THE BOOK

In the process of conducting research for this book, I quickly realized the difficulty of telling the story, even by relying on photographs to convey the proverbial thousand words. The magnitude of the events and the period of time during which they occurred resisted condensing. Others before me, more learned and experienced, had faced similar obstacles. Following the war, a number of MFAA officers and other heroes (such as Rose Valland, the brave young woman who risked her life to create a secret tracking inventory of stolen works from Paris collections) recounted their own experiences. Many are enjoyable—even exciting—to read, but most deal with a limited portion of the much larger story. Certainly Janet Flanner's series of articles written for *The New Yorker* in 1947 provide an excellent overview of Hitler's ambitious plans for his museum complex in Linz, Austria, and compelling descriptions of various German officials' looting activities. However, not until the 1994 publishing of Lynn Nicholas's book, *The Rape of Europa: The Fate of Europe's Treasures in the Third Reich and the Second World War*, was the complete story of the role of art in Nazi Germany, Hitler's determination to plunder Europe's greatest art treasures for his museum in Linz, and the premeditated and skilled organization the Nazis created to fulfill these objectives so thoroughly explained.

Numerous other books and papers have since been published on the topic, many of which have a narrow, single-subject focus. Some are scholarly in nature, others more anecdotal. Excellent, thorough research and writing by scholars and historians such as Jonathan Petropoulos (*Art as Politics in the Third Reich*, *The Faustian Bargain: The Art World of Nazi Germany*), Stephanie Barron (*Degenerate Art*), Nancy Yeide (*AAM Guide to Provenance Research*), and Birgit Schwarz (*Hitlers Museum*), among others, have provided further insight into that incredible time. Each looted piece of art that finds its way "home" has a beneficiary who owes these and other scholars a huge debt of gratitude. Their work illuminated the path.

After studying almost every book I could find on the subject, in addition to the forty-four-volume transcript of the Nuremberg trials, I concluded that no one book can cover all that occurred in each country during such a prolonged period.

This book is an effort to convey the magnitude of the story using period photographs of locations and artwork of greatest familiarity. The decision to exclude coverage of events in any particular country, city, or institution was a consequence of limited time and space only, not a slight or inference that others weren't just as severely impacted.

NOTE ABOUT THE PHOTOGRAPHS

The photographs in this book come from archives in the United States and various countries throughout Western and Eastern Europe, as well as private collections. The excellent photographic documentation of these events is largely attributable to the United States Army Signal Corps, Monuments, Fine Arts, and Archives officers, and, ironically, Heinrich Hoffmann, Hitler's personal photographer. Among other duties, the Signal Corps played a key role in coordinating timely and accurate information concerning all military units in the European theater to army and civilian personnel. Their photographic documentation of combat missions and other significant events during and after the war was an invaluable record of Allied activities. Monuments officers were responsible for protecting cultural and artistic treasures, tracking down missing works of art, and ultimately returning them to the owners or their representatives. Many of these individuals' personal accounts and photographic records, especially of the astonishing discoveries involving the stolen works of art, provide the most riveting account of these events. In contrast, Hoffman's work was a consequence of Hitler's abiding ego and his desire to control where and how photographs of him were taken. These records became the property of the United States government and are now stored in the National Archives and Records Administration in College Park, Maryland.

In many instances, the captions that accompany each photograph merely explain the subject matter and context in which it was taken. They are my words. In other instances, I have taken the opportunity to provide a description using the words of others. Each instance has been duly noted. Some of the words come from journalists, others participants. Many were observers caught up in events not of their choosing. They were there; they witnessed; they experienced the events. Combining their words with the photographs comes as close as possible to recreating that particular moment in time.

Photograph Credits

Every effort possible was made to identify the current copyright owner of each image used in this book. However, given the passage of time since these events, and changes in ownership of the images during the last sixty years, errors may have occurred. Should you identify such an error and wish to provide the correct information, please contact me at rmedsel@rescuingdavinci.com.

AAN, Warsaw (Archiwum Akt Nowych) 92 (below), 274 (center)

ADM, Warsaw (Archiwum Dokumentacji Mechanicznej) 89 (right, left), 90 (left), 91 (above, below), 272 (above), 274 (above), 275

AKG-Images 97

Alfred Jonniaux (artist), Collection of the Supreme Court of the United States 148d

Alinari 76 (above left)

Alinari/Art Resource, NY 215 (above), 233 (below)

AP 99 (below), 186-87

Archiv der Stadt Linz, Fotosammlung 30 (below)

Artothek 265 (below)

Bavarian State Library, Munich 34 (below), 35 (below), 42 (above), 43 (above)

Bayerisches Hauptstaatsarchiv, NL - Hitler - 38 30 (above)

Bernard Taper 146d

Bildarchiv Preussischer Kulturbesitz, Berlin 17 (above, below), 96, 281 (below)

Bildarchiv Preussischer Kulturbesitz/Art Resource, NY 167, 282 (below left and right), 283 (below)

Bundesarchiv 4 (below), 43 (below), 60 (below), 100, 116 (above, center, below)

Civici Musei Udine 76 (above right)

CJ Fox (artist), Collection of the Supreme Court of the United States 148e

Czartoryski Museum, Cracow iv, 251

David de Rothschild 202 (above)

Deane Keller Papers, Manuscripts & Archives, Yale University Library 70 (above), 157 (below), 230 (below), 234 (below)

Dokumentationsarchiv Österreichischer Widerstand 193 (below), 202 (below)

Erich Lessing/Art Resource, NY xi, 205, 215 (below), 249

Franklin D. Roosevelt Presidential Library, reproduction of original presidential proclamation to City of Leningrad, signed by President Roosevelt, May 17, 1944, From Official File 220 (Russia), 1944-1945 256

Fred Ramage/Hulton Archive/Getty Images 52 (below)

Führer's Favorite Museum, following p. 96 36 (lower right)

Harry L. Ettlinger 145d, 145e

Harvard University Archives (Call # UAV 874.1269) 151

Hugo Jaeger/Time Life Pictures/Getty Images 16

Institute of Art, Polish Academy of Science, Warsaw 144e, 273 (left)

Kenneth C. Lindsay, Professor Emeritus 18, 29, 145f, 146a

Kings College Archive Centre, Cambridge, The Papers of Ronald Edmund Balfour, Misc. 5/9 150

Le Monnier, Florence xii, 72 (above), 74 (lower left)

Library of Congress, Washington D.C. 19 (above), 40, 41 (below), 44 (above, below), 82, 113

© Luce Institute 74 (above left), 104, 120-21

Lynn Nicholas Collection 19 (lower right), 26, 27, 36 (lower left), 55 (left), 79 (above, below), 102 (below), 109, 115 (center), 117, 142d, 144a, 145c, 146e, 146f, 147a, 147b, 147d, 155 (below), 171, 174, 181 (below), 189 (above), 192 (above), 194-95, 216 (above), 236, 250 (center), 282 (above), 283 (above)

Lynn Nicholas Collection, courtesy of the Walker Hancock Family 126, 138 (above, below), 143d, 162 (above left)

Lynn Nicholas Collection/Craig Hugh Smyth 143b, 143c, 148a, 148c, 198, 210 (above, below), 211 (below), 212 (above left and right, below), 213, 226, 244 (above, center, below)

Lynn Nicholas Collection/Klaus Goldmann 163 (above)

Marc Vaux/Centre Georges Pompidou 58 (below)

Meadows Museums Southern Methodist University, Dallas, Algur H. Meadows Collection 182 (below), 215 (center)

Muzeum Narodowe, Warsaw, Poland, Giraudon/Bridgeman Art Library 273 (above)

National Archives and Records Administration, College Park, MD vi, viii (right), xvi, 13, 19 (lower left), 20 (above, below), 22 (above, below), 34 (above), 41 (above), 45 (above, below), 46-47, 59, 63 (center, below left and right), 64 (above, below), 65, 72 (below), 73, 75, 92 (above), 93 (above, below), 95, 108, 111 (left, right), 112 (above, below), 118 (above, below), 122 (above), 130, 131, 132, 133, 134 (left, right), 135, 136, 137, 139 (above, below), 140, 142b, 142c, 142e, 143a, 144c, 146b, 146c, 148b, 152, 154 (right), 155 (above), 157 (above), 160 (above, below), 161, 162 (above right, below), 163 (below), 164 (above, below), 165, 166, 168-69, 170, 172 (above, below), 176 (above, below), 178 (above, below), 181 (above), 183, 184-85, 189 (below), 190, 191, 192 (below), 196 (below), 199 (below), 218, 220, 222, 223, 224 (above, center, below), 225, 230 (above), 232 (right), 234 (above), 235 (above, center, below), 237 (above, center, left, below left), 238 (above right), 242-43, 245 (above right and left), 246 (above, below left and right), 247, 248 (left, right, below), 250 (below), 253, 262, 263 (above, below left), 264 (above, below), 265 (above), 266 (below left and right), 267 (above left and right, below), 268 (above left, below), 269 (above, below), 270-71, 276, 277, 278, 279

National Gallery of Art, Washington D.C., Gallery Archives **xiii, xiv, 83, 84** (above, below), **85, 119, 123** (above, below), **142a, 144b, 144d, 145a, 145b, 147c, 154** (left), **179, 180** (left, right), **182** (above), **196** (above), **204** (above), **209** (above, below), **211** (above), **214, 216** (below left and right), **217, 221** (above left and right, below), **232** (above, below left), **234** (center) **240** (above, below), **250** (above), **266** (above)

National Gallery of Art, Washington, D.C.: Photograph courtesy of the Department of Image Collections, National Gallery of Art Library, Washington, D.C., from the collection of the National Archives at College Park, MD, Record Group 260 (photograph nos. 260-MP-146-9, 260-MP-2609/1, 260-MP-4364, 260-MP-1588, 260-MP-1580/1, 260-MP-8051, 260-MP-8047, 260-MP-4362, 260-MP-146-15) **107** (photos only)

National Gallery, London **50-51, 53** (above and below)

National Gallery, London, © National Railway Museum / Science & Society Picture Library **52** (above left and right)

National Museum of the U.S. Army, Army Art Collection **28** (above, below)

Nebraska State Historical Society Photograph Collections **245** (below)

Paul Maeyaert/Bridgeman Art Library **173**

Pierre Jahan/Roger-Viollet **58** (above), **238** (above left, below left and right)

© Reproductiefonds/photo Hugo Maertens **200-01**

Research Library, The Getty Research Institute, Los Angeles (840001) **23** (below)

Research Library, The Getty Research Institute, Los Angeles (89.P.4) **23** (center), **42** (below), **206, 241** (above)

Réunion des Musées Nationaux/Art Resource, NY **54, 203, 239**

Rijksmuseum, Amsterdam **62** (above, center, below), **63** (above), **66-67**

Robert M. Edsel Collection **122** (lower right), **257** (above left and right, below), **263** (below right), **272** (below), **273** (below right), **274** (below)

Robert M. Edsel Collection, courtesy of Wawel Castle, Cracow **110** (above left and right, below)

Robert M. Edsel Collection, photograph by Andrzej Lewandowski, courtesy of Czartoryski Museum, Cracow **284**

Rotterdam Municipal Archives **94**

Royal Castle Archives, Warsaw **90** (right), **272** (center)

Scala/Art Resource, NY **vi** (above), **viii** (left), **70** (below), **156, 158-59, 197, 219** (above right), **231** (left and right), **233** (above)

SEF/Art Resource, NY **74** (lower right)

Service des bibliotheques, des archives et de la documentation generale des Musées de France **55** (right), **56, 57, 60** (above), **61** (above, center, below), **114** (above, below), **115** (above, below)

Snark/Art Resource, NY **ii**

Soprintendenza Speciale per il Polo Museale Fiorentino— Gabinetto Fotografico—Su concessione del Ministero per i Beni e le Attività Culturali (Florence) **68, 69, 71** (left, right), **122** (lower left), **258**

Soprintendenza Speciale per il Polo Museale Veneziano— Archivio Fotografico—Su concessione del Ministero per i Beni e le Attività Culturali (Venice) **76** (below), **77** (above, below)

Sovfoto **124, 252** (above left), **254, 288**

Staatliche Kunsthalle Karlsruhe **175** (above, below left and right), **177**

© The State Hermitage Museum, St. Petersburg **80** (above, below), **81, 102** (above left and right)

TASS/Sovfoto **78** (above), **252** (above right)

© Topham/The Image Works **188, 193** (above), **199** (top), **204** (below)

The Art Newspaper, headlines compiled by author **286-87**

The John Nicholas Brown Center for the Study of American Civilization **144e**

The Petersburg State Archive of Photo and Film Documents **78** (below), **103, 252** (below)

The State Museum-Preserve "Tsarskoye Selo" **125** (above, below), **288-89**

© The State Pushkin Museum of Fine Arts, Moscow **255** (above, below)

Ullstein Bild **1, 2, 3, 4** (above), **5, 6-7, 8, 14-15, 23** (above), **24-25, 35** (above), **36** (above), **37, 86, 101, 261, 268** (above right), **280**

Ullstein Bild/SV-Bilderdienst **98, 99** (above), **281** (above)

Ullstein Bild/Walter Frentz **21, 31** (above), **32, 38, 39**

Vanni/Art Resource, NY **74** (above right), **241** (below)

© Walter Frentz Collection, Berlin **31** (center, below), **33**

Wittelsbacher Ausgleichsfonds, Munich, image provided by Artothek **219** (above left, below)

Maps on inside cover pages and opposite the half-title page were designed by Blue Marble Maps LLC, with images from: Alinari/Art Resource NY, Czartoryski Museum, Cracow, Dokumentationsarchiv Österreichischer Widerstand, Erich Lessing/Art Resource NY, Lynn Nicholas Collection/Klaus Goldmann, Lynn Nicholas Collection, National Archives and Records Administration, College Park, MD. National Gallery, London, Scala/Art Resource, NY, National Gallery of Art, Washington D.C., Gallery Archives, Réunion des Musées Nationaux/Art Resource, NY.

INDEX

DO YOU HAVE A CONNECTION TO THIS STORY?

...LAWRENCE OF ARABIA DID

This photograph, taken between 1911 and 1914, shows Sir Thomas Edward Lawrence—more commonly known as Lawrence of Arabia—standing to the left of a Hittite slab found at an excavation at Carchemish, near Aleppo, Syria. The man on the right is Sir Charles Leonard Woolley, a distinguished British archaeologist who would later become an instrumental figure in the early work of the MFAA in recovering the looted art treasures of Europe during World War II.

Hitler's looting of art and the Allies' rescue of it is the single most extraordinary "untold" story of World War II.

It is an important story whose telling is another and perhaps more interesting way to learn about art, travel, and history. Publishing this book and co-producing the film are two methods of "telling the story" that we know; creation of our website is a path to learning that which we don't.

Our website is designed to connect the broadest number of people to this story by allowing for an exchange of information. At the site you will see additional photographs and other information not included in the limited pages of this book. But there is also an opportunity for you to provide us with new information about events you or a family member may possess. Perhaps you know a sensitive piece of information that needs an anonymous forum. Or maybe you have old photographs of these events you would like to share with us. Possibly you know of someone not on our list of "Heroes and Heroines" (see Chapter 5) who served in the MFAA section during the war. We are interested in this information and will post it to our site, as appropriate.

Find more information—or provide some—at www.rescuingdavinci.com.

The Rape of Europa is a two-hour documentary film produced by Actual Films based on Lynn Nicholas' detailed account. Narrated by acclaimed actress Joan Allen, it includes moving interviews with key Monuments Men and a variety of museum officials. Shot on location in Europe, Russia, and the United States, it contrasts the beauty of museums such as the Hermitage and Louvre to the ugly memories of why the salt mines of Alt Aussee were used by Hitler, Göring, and the Nazis. While the film provides an historical account of these events, it also profiles the current story that continues to unfold.

Find more information about the film and its public release at www.rapeofeuropa.com.

North
Sea

RUSSIA

LENINGRAD
(ST. PETERSBUR

ENGLAND

LONDON

BELGIUM

COMPIÈGNE

PARIS

VADUZ

GERMANY

BERLIN

WARSAW

POLAND

CRACOW

MUNICH

LINZ

VIENNA

ALT AUSSEE

SWITZ.

AUSTRIA

MILAN

FRANCE

ITALY

FLORENCE

ROME

NAPLES